Life Hungers To Abound

POEMS OF THE FAMILY

LIFE HUNGERS
TO ABOUND

 *Poems of the Family*

Selected by HELEN PLOTZ

GREENWILLOW BOOKS
A Division of William Morrow & Company, Inc.
New York

In memory of Milton
and of our parents
  ⚜ *Hyman and Ethel Ratnoff*
  ⚜ *Isaac and Rose Plotz*

First Edition   10 9 8 7 6 5 4 3 2 1

Library of Congress Cataloging in Publication Data
Main entry under title: Life hungers to abound.
Includes indexes.
Summary: A collection of poems concerned with
aspects of family life including relationships among
members, divorce, happiness, and sorrow.
1. Family—Juvenile poetry. [1. Family life—Poetry.
2. American poetry—Collections]   I. Plotz, Helen.
PN6110.C4L47   811'.008'035   78-5829
ISBN 0-688-80176-5
ISBN 0-688-84176-7 lib. bdg.

CONTENTS

INTRODUCTION

"Happy families are all alike; every unhappy family is unhappy in its own way." This famous untruism has been bandied about for a hundred years, and for a hundred years some of us have accepted it without stopping to think what it means. In truth, happy families, as most of us know, are as different from each other as unhappy families. Although the family without problems exists only in the Dick and Jane stories (and what bores they are), nevertheless there are countless families whose members are bound to each other by ties of love, of understanding and of loyalty. Indeed, the deep joys of family life have been celebrated again and again in our literature and especially in our poetry.

If happy families are not alike, neither are unhappy families, though one might make a case for a reversal of the axiom which I have quoted. Unhappiness is indubitably intensified by the existence of family ties, unwelcome or oppressive though they may be. The tragedy of divorce is in direct proportion to the hopes of marriage; the sorrows following the alienation of brothers and sisters and of parents and children are immeasurable.

As to unhappy families, I shall not venture a definition. It would seem that every conflict in the world can exist in the family and that every Commandment can be broken and every deadly sin committed within the confines of the family. Not by chance did the Mark of Cain become part of our language; not by chance are we gripped by Medea, by Electra and by Oedipus, by Hamlet, by King Lear and by Othello.

If we think of Abraham and Isaac, David and Absalom, Ruth and Naomi, Jephthah and his daughter, the Holy Family, the Prodigal Son, and Martha and Mary, we see love and rivalry and sacrifice vividly and unforgettably portrayed.

The family as we know it in our civilization is almost as it was described in Biblical days and in the Greek tragedies which have come down to us. Many other civilizations have different patterns, but in the Western world we follow the ancient way of the Old and New Testaments and of the Greeks.

There is much jargon today about the "nuclear" and the "extended" family and much concern about the disappearance of the extended family; that is, of grandparents, uncles, aunts, and cousins as part of the child's experience. This concern is understandable when we consider how many families are scattered to the four winds—by choice or by necessity. In fact, however, many young pioneer families and young immigrants of former times often left their parents and grandparents behind when they moved into new territory. Still, we tend to think of the American Family as always having been gathered round the Thanksgiving table with three or even four generations sharing in a family reunion. Whether this traditional pattern can continue, I do not know. It is more than sentimentality or nostalgia that prompts our interest in the extended family, and there is something both pathetic and disturbing (to the older generation, that is) in the "new" families arranged by some of our young people.

The poems in this book are concerned with aspects of family life, that is to say, with aspects of all of life. They deal with divorce and estrangement as well as with joy and fulfillment. The divisions are not fixed; it is impossible to categorize this most complex, most difficult and most rewarding subject. If mothers and fathers could exist without children, children without parents, ancestors without descendants, then perhaps I could arrange these poems more neatly. Fortunately, I cannot.

I have arranged the poems in five groups—very loosely. The groups are: first, marriage. Then, parents speaking to and about their children. The third section includes brothers and sisters. The fourth, which I have called ancestors and descendants, contains poems about grandparents, remote ancestors, uncles, aunts and cousins. Last and most moving of all are the poems in which children speak to their parents, sometimes in deep love and gratitude, sometimes begging forgiveness for the years of unawareness, and often calling out to the parent, now dead, whose life has illumined the life of the child.

> One generation passeth away,
> and another generation cometh:
> but the earth abideth for ever.
> *Ecclesiastes 1:4*

MARRIAGE

Therefore shall a man leave his father
and his mother, and shall cleave unto
his wife: and they shall be one flesh.

Genesis 2:24

And God said, Let us make man in our image, after our likeness: and let them have dominion over the fish of the sea, and over the fowl of the air, and over the cattle, and over all the earth, and over every creeping thing that creepeth upon the earth.

So God created man in his *own* image, in the image of God created he him; male and female created he them.

And God blessed them, and God said unto them, Be fruitful, and multiply, and replenish the earth, and subdue it: and have dominion over the fish of the sea, and over the fowl of the air, and over every living thing that moveth upon the earth.

GENESIS 1:26-28

from *PARADISE LOST*

Two of far nobler shape, erect and tall,
God-like erect, with native honour clad
In naked majesty, seemed lords of all,
And worthy seemed; for in their looks divine
The image of their glorious Maker shon,
Truth, wisdom, sanctitude severe and pure—
Severe, but in true filial freedom placed,
Whence true authority in men: though both
Not equal, as their sex not equal seemed;
For contemplation he and valour formed,
For softness she and sweet attractive grace;
He for God only, she for God in him.
His fair large front and eye sublime declared
Absolute rule.

JOHN MILTON

Thus piteously Love closed what he begat:
The union of this ever-diverse pair!
These two were rapid falcons in a snare,
Condemned to do the flitting of the bat.
Lovers beneath the singing sky of May,
They wandered once; clear as the dew on flowers:
But they fed not on the advancing hours:
Their hearts held cravings for the buried day.
Then each applied to each that fatal knife,
Deep questioning, which probes to endless dole.
Ah, what a dusty answer gets the soul
When hot for certainties in this our life!—
In tragic hints here see what evermore
Moves dark as yonder midnight ocean's force,
Thundering like ramping hosts of warrior horse,
To throw that faint thin line upon the shore!

GEORGE MEREDITH

Let me not to the marriage of true minds
Admit impediments. Love is not love
Which alters when it alteration finds,
Or bends with the remover to remove:
O, no! it is an ever-fixed mark,
That looks on tempests and is never shaken;
It is the star to every wandering bark,
Whose worth's unknown, although his height be taken.
Love's not Time's fool, though rosy lips and cheeks
Within his bending sickle's compass come;
Love alters not with his brief hours and weeks,
But bears it out even to the edge of doom.
   If this be error and upon me proved,
   I never writ, nor no man ever loved.

WILLIAM SHAKESPEARE

LET ME LIVE WITH MARRIAGE

Let me live with marriage
as unruly as alive
or else alone and longing
not too long alone.
Love if unduly held by guilt
is guilty with fear
wronging that fixed impulse
to seek and ever more
to bind with love. Oh yes!
I am black within
as is this skin
without one pore
to bleed a pale defense: Will you attack
as cruel
as you claim me cruel? With word with silence
I have flung myself from you. And now
absurd
I sing of stillborn lyrics almost sung.

If this be baffling then the error's proved
To love so long and leave my love unmoved.

JUNE JORDAN

THE OLD FLAME

My old flame, my wife!
Remember our lists of birds?
One morning last summer, I drove
by our house in Maine. It was still
on top of its hill—

Now a red ear of Indian maize
was splashed on the door.
Old Glory with thirteen stripes
hung on a pole. The clapboard
was old-red schoolhouse red.

Inside, a new landlord,
a new wife, a new broom!
Atlantic seaboard antique shop
pewter and plunder
shone in each room.

A new frontier!
No running next door
now to phone the sheriff
for his taxi to Bath
and the State Liquor Store!

No one saw your ghostly
imaginary lover
stare through the window,
and tighten
the scarf at his throat.

Health to the new people,
health to their flag, to their old
restored house on the hill!
Everything had been swept bare,
furnished, garnished and aired.

Everything's changed for the best—
how quivering and fierce we were,
there snowbound together,
simmering like wasps
in our tent of books!

Poor ghost, old love, speak
with your old voice
of flaming insight
that kept us awake all night.
In one bed and apart,

we heard the plow
groaning up hill—
a red light, then a blue,
as it tossed off the snow
to the side of the road.

ROBERT LOWELL

9

HUSBAND, HUSBAND, CEASE YOUR STRIFE

I

"Husband, husband, cease your strife,
    Nor longer idly rave, sir!
Tho' I am your wedded wife,
    Yet I am not your slave, sir."
"One of two must still obey,
    Nancy, Nancy!
Is it Man or Woman, say,
    My spouse Nancy?"

II

"If 't is still the lordly word,
    Service and obedience,
I'll desert my sov'reign lord,
    And so goodbye, allegiance!"
"Sad will I be so bereft,
    Nancy, Nancy!
Yet I'll try to make a shift,
    My spouse Nancy!"

III

"My poor heart, then break it must,
    My last hour I am near it:
When you lay me in the dust,
    Think, how will you bear it?"
"I will hope and trust in Heaven,
    Nancy, Nancy!
Strength to bear it will be given,
    My spouse Nancy."

IV
"Well, sir, from the silent dead,
    Still I'll try to daunt you:
Ever round your midnight bed
    Horrid sprites shall haunt you!"
"I'll wed another like my dear,
    Nancy, Nancy!
Then all Hell will fly for fear,
    My spouse Nancy!"

ROBERT BURNS

NATURAL TEARS

After such years of dissension and strife,
Some wonder that Peter should weep for his wife:
But his tears on her grave are nothing surprising—
He's laying her dust, for fear of its rising.

THOMAS HOOD

EPIGRAM ON MY WEDDING-DAY

To Penelope

This day, of all our days, has done
    The worst for me and you: —
Tis just *six* years since we were *one*,
    And *five* since we were *two*.

GEORGE GORDON, LORD BYRON

MAG

I wish to God I never saw you, Mag.
I wish you never quit your job and came along with me.
I wish we never bought a licence and a white dress
For you to get married in the day we ran off to a minister
And told him we would love each other and take care of
    each other
Always and always long as the sun and the rain lasts
    anywhere.
Yes, I'm wishing now you lived somewhere away from
    here
And I was a bum on the bumpers a thousand miles away
    dead broke.
  I wish the kids had never come
  And rent and coal and clothes to pay for
  And a grocery man calling for cash,
  Every day cash for beans and prunes.
  I wish to God I never saw you, Mag.
  I wish to God the kids had never come.

CARL SANDBURG

MEMENTOS, 1

Sorting out letters and piles of my old
    Canceled checks, old clippings, and yellow note cards
That meant something once, I happened to find
    Your picture. *That* picture. I stopped there cold,
Like a man raking piles of dead leaves in his yard
       Who has turned up a severed hand.

Still, that first second, I was glad: you stand
    Just as you stood—shy, delicate, slender,
In that long gown of green lace netting and daisies
    That you wore to our first dance. The sight of you
       stunned
Us all. Well, our needs were different, then,
       And our ideals came easy.

Then through the war and those two long years
    Overseas, the Japanese dead in their shacks
Among dishes, dolls, and lost shoes; I carried
    This glimpse of you, there, to choke down my fear,
Prove it had been, that it might come back.
       That was before we got married.

—Before we drained out one another's force
    With lies, self-denial, unspoken regret
And the sick eyes that blame; before the divorce
    And the treachery. Say it: before we met. Still,
I put back your picture. Someday, in due course,
       I will find that it's still there.

W. D. SNODGRASS

OLD AND NEW

Anonymous (first century B.C.)

She went up the mountain to pluck wild herbs;
She came down the mountain and met her former
    husband.
She knelt down and asked her former husband
"What do you find your new wife like?"
"My new wife, although her talk is clever,
Cannot charm me as my old wife could.
In beauty of face there is not much to choose,
But in usefulness they are not at all alike.
My new wife comes in from the road to meet me;
My old wife always came down from her tower.
My new wife is clever at embroidering silk;
My old wife was good at plain sewing.
Of silk embroidery one can do an inch a day;
Of plain sewing, more than five feet.
Putting her silks by the side of your sewing,
I see that the new will not compare with the old."

Translated by Arthur Waley

OVER THE COFFIN

They stand confronting, the coffin between,
His wife of old, and his wife of late,
And the dead man whose they both had been
Seems listening aloof, as to things past date.
—"I have called," says the first.
         "Do you marvel or not?"
"In truth," says the second, "I do—somewhat."

"Well, there was a word to be said by me! . . .
I divorced that man because of you—
It seemed I must do it, boundenly;
But now I am older, and tell you true,
For life is little, and dead lies he;
I would I had let alone you two!
And both of us, scorning parochial ways,
Had lived like the wives in the patriarchs' days."

THOMAS HARDY

TWO STRANGERS BREAKFAST

The law says you and I belong to each other, George.
The law says you are mine and I am yours, George.
And there are a million miles of white snowstorms, a
     million furnaces of hell,
Between the chair where you sit and the chair where I sit.
The law says two strangers shall eat breakfast together
     after nights on the horn of an Arctic moon.

CARL SANDBURG

LOSS

Immeasurably sad, O long ago
she ceased her being with mine, mine like a fuse
sputtering toward a common doom.
She said in her heart "I must create my own."
I learn this now on a mild & terrible morning.

Too late—too far distrust & guilt & pain
too late for any return or any beginning
of any nearness or hope again.
All desire's blown out of me by loss,
an aching backward only, dull, of our marvellous love.

JOHN BERRYMAN

She rose to His Requirement—dropt
The Playthings of Her Life
To take the honorable Work
Of Woman, and of Wife—

If ought She missed in Her new Day,
Of Amplitude, or Awe—
Or first Prospective—Or the Gold
In using, wear away,

It lay unmentioned—as the Sea
Develop Pearl, and Weed,
But only to Himself—be known
The Fathoms they abide—

EMILY DICKINSON

PRAISE OF A GOOD WOMAN

Who can find a virtuous woman?
For her price *is* far above rubies.
The heart of her husband doth safely trust in her,
so that he shall have no need of spoil.
She will do him good and not evil
all the days of her life.
She seeketh wool, and flax,
and worketh willingly with her hands.
She is like the merchants' ships;
she bringeth her food from afar.
She riseth also while it is yet night,
and giveth meat to her household,
and a portion to her maidens.
She considereth a field, and buyeth it:
with the fruit of her hands she planteth a vineyard.
She girdeth her loins with strength
and strengtheneth her arms.
She perceiveth that her merchandise *is* good:
her candle goeth not out by night.
She layeth her hands to the spindle,
and her hands hold the distaff.
She stretcheth out her hand to the poor;
yea, she reacheth forth her hands to the needy.
She is not afraid of the snow for her household:
for all her household *are* clothed with scarlet.
She maketh herself coverings of tapestry;
her clothing *is* silk and purple.
Her husband is known in the gates,
when he sitteth among the elders of the land.
She maketh fine linen, and selleth *it;*
and delivereth girdles unto the merchant.

Strength and honor *are* her clothing;
and she shall rejoice in time to come.
She openeth her mouth with wisdom;
and in her tongue *is* the law of kindness.
She looketh well to the ways of her household,
and eateth not the bread of idleness.
Her children arise up, and call her blessed;
her husband *also*, and he praiseth her.
Many daughters have done virtuously,
but thou excellest them all.
Favor *is* deceitful and beauty *is* vain:
but a woman *that* feareth the Lord, she shall be praised.
Give her of the fruit of her hands;
and let her own works praise her in the gates.

PROVERBS 31:10-31

TO MY DEAR AND LOVING HUSBAND

If ever two were one, then surely we.
If ever man were lov'd by wife, then thee.
If ever wife was happy in a man,
Compare with me, ye women, if you can.
I prize thy love more than whole Mines of gold,
Or all the riches that the East doth hold.
My love is such that Rivers cannot quench,
Nor ought but love from thee give recompence.
Thy love is such I can no way repay;
The heavens reward thee manifold I pray.
Then while we live, in love lets so persever,
That when we live no more, we may live ever.

ANNE BRADSTREET

JOHN ANDERSON MY JO

I

John Anderson my jo, John,
  When we were first acquent,
Your locks were like the raven,
  Your bonie brow was brent;*
But now your brow is beld, John,
  Your locks are like the snaw,
But blessings on your frosty pow,
  John Anderson my jo!

II

John Anderson my jo, John,
  We clamb the hill thegither,
And monie a cantie† day, John,
  We've had wi' ane anither;
Now we maun totter down, John,
  And hand in hand we'll go,
And sleep thegither at the foot,
  John Anderson my jo!

ROBERT BURNS

---

*brent: smooth
†cantie: pleasant

TO HIS WIFE

Beware, my love, lest you should see,
Vassal of too indulgent eyes,
The hero's gaze victorious
Become above the morning tea
(Ex-Cortez with a lost surmise)
Merely a smile uxorious.

THEODORE SPENCER

from SONNETS TO THE PORTUGUESE

Unlike are we, unlike, O princely Heart!
Unlike our uses and our destinies.
Our ministering two angels look surprise
On one another, as they strike athwart
Their wings in passing. Thou, bethink thee, art
A quest for queens to social pageantries,
With gages from a hundred brighter eyes
Than tears even can make mine, to play thy part
Of chief musician. What hast *thou* to do
With looking from the lattice-lights at me,
A poor, tired, wandering singer, singing through
The dark, and leaning up a cypress tree?
The chrism is on thine head,—on mine, the dew,—
And Death must dig the level where these agree.

ELIZABETH BARRETT BROWNING

from *TO E. B. B.*

What were seen? None knows, none ever shall know.
Only this is sure—the sight were other,
Not the moon's same side, born late in Florence,
Dying now impoverished here in London.
God be thanked, the meanest of his creatures
Boasts two soul-sides, one to face the world with,
One to show a woman when he loves her!

This I say of me, but think of you, Love!
This to you—yourself my moon of poets!
Ah, but that's the world's side, there's the wonder,
Thus they see you, praise you, think they know you!
There, in turn I stand with them and praise you—
Out of my own self, I dare to phrase it.
But the best is when I glide from out them,
Cross a step or two of dubious twilight,
Come out on the other side, the novel
Silent silver lights and darks undreamed of,
Where I hush and bless myself with silence.

ROBERT BROWNING

27

HUSBAND AND WIFE

I wonder why you said to me in your dream,
Eight years after our wedding, "Let's get married."
The grace of blindness leaves me free to guess.
Was it refreshment simply, at the stream
Of our first pleasure? A gentle, harried
Plea? Or a cunning emblem of success?

You tell me the dream: you joke about it and then
Forget: why drill for logic in the second
Of those alternatives? The first is trite.
The third proclaims your shrewdness about men,
How calm and gay your love, how well you reckoned
Possible ironies, tricks of appetite.

Married-love should be spelt with capital letters
Only in dreams: is asked for only there
Except by the wistful. Marriage awake is not
The loving, but the loving with all its fetters:
Aphrodite with curlers in her hair;
The house, the job, the pram, the garden plot.

In waking, then, most wisely you pretend
(This much your dream implies) we are not more
Than friends and lovers: keep my touching new,
My tender lust alight. The coin we spend,
Worn smooth, retains its worth: in dreams you store
Inviolate gold. I'm glad I married you.

RICHARD KELL

UNFINISHED HISTORY

We have loved each other in this time twenty years
And with such love as few men have in them even for
One or for the marriage month or the hearing of

Three nights' carts in the street but it will leave them.
We have been lovers the twentieth year now:
Our bed has been made in many houses and evenings.

The apple-tree moves at the window in this house:
There were palms rattled the night through in one:
In one there were red tiles and the sea's hours.

We have made our bed in the changes of many months—
The light of the day is still overlong in the windows
Till night shall bring us the lamp and one another.

Those that have seen her have no thought what she is:
Her face is clear in the sun as a palmful of water:
Only by night and in love are the dark winds on it. . . .

I wrote this poem that day when I thought
Since we have loved we two so long together
Shall we have done together—all love gone?

Or how then will it change with us when the breath
Is no more able for such joy and the blood is
Thin in the throat and the time not come for death?

ARCHIBALD MAC LEISH

THE MARRIAGE

Incarnate for our marriage you appeared,
Flesh living in the spirit and endeared
By minor graces and slow sensual change.
Through every nerve we made our spirits range.
We fed our minds on every mortal thing:
The lacy fronds of carrots in the spring,
Their flesh sweet on the tongue, the salty wine
From bitter grapes, which gathered through the vine
The mineral drouth of autumn concentrate,
Wild spring in dream escaping, the debate
Of flesh and spirit on those vernal nights,
Its resolution in naive delights,
The young kids bleating softly in the rain—
All this to pass, not to return again.
And when I found your flesh did not resist,
It was the living spirit that I kissed,
It was the spirit's change in which I lay:
Thus, mind in mind we waited for the day.
When flesh shall fall away, and, falling, stand
Wrinkling with shadow over face and hand,
Still I shall meet you on the verge of dust
And know you as a faithful vestige must.
And, in commemoration of our lust,
May our heirs seal us in a single urn,
A single spirit never to return.

YVOR WINTERS

AN EPITAPH UPON
HUSBAND AND WIFE, WHICH DIED,
AND WERE BURIED TOGETHER

To these whom death again did wed
This grave's the second marriage-bed.
For though the hand of fate could force
'Twixt soul and body a divorce,
It could not sunder man and wife,
'Cause they both lived but one life.
Peace, good reader. Do not weep.
Peace, the lovers are asleep.
They, sweet turtles, folded lie
In the last knot love could tie.
And though they lie as they were dead,
Their pillow stone, their sheets of lead
(Pillow hard, and sheets not warm),
Love made the bed: they'll take no harm.
Let them sleep, let them sleep on
Till this stormy night be gone,
Till the eternal morrow dawn.
Then the curtains will be drawn,
And they wake into a light
Whose day shall never die in night.

RICHARD CRASHAW

A VALEDICTION:
FORBIDDING MOURNING

As virtuous men pass mildly away,
   And whisper to their souls, to go,
Whilst some of their sad friends do say,
   The breath goes now, and some say, no:

So let us melt, and make no noise,
   No tear-floods, nor sigh-tempests move,
'Twere profanation of our joys
   To tell the laity our love.

Moving of th' earth brings harms and fears,
   Men reckon what it did and meant,
But trepidation of the spheres,
   Though greater far, is innocent.

Dull sublunary lovers' love
   (Whose soul is sense) cannot admit
Absence, because it doth remove
   Those things which elemented it.

But we by a love, so much refin'd,
   That ourselves know not what it is,
Inter-assurèd of the mind,
   Care less eyes, lips, and hands to miss.

Our two souls therefore, which are one,
   Though I must go, endure not yet
A breach, but an expansion,
   Like gold to aery thinness beat.

Donne wrote this poem for his wife on his going abroad.

If they be two, they are two so
    As stiff twin compasses are two,
Thy soul the fixed foot, makes no show
    To move, but doth, if th' other do.

And though it in the centre sit,
    Yet when the other far doth roam,
It leans, and hearkens after it,
    And grows erect, as that comes home.

Such wilt thou be to me, who must
    Like th' other foot, obliquely run;
Thy firmness draws my circle just,
    And makes me end, where I begun.

JOHN DONNE

DRAFTED

They married us when they put
Up our hair. We were just twenty
And fifteen. And ever since,
Our love has never been troubled.
Tonight we have the old joy
In each other, although our
Happiness will soon be over.
I remember the long march
That lies ahead of me, and
Go out and look up at the stars,
To see how the night has worn on.
Betelgeuse and Antares
Have both gone out. It is time
For me to leave for far off
Battlefields. No way of knowing
If we will ever see each
Other again. We clutch each
Other and sob, our faces
Streaming with tears. Goodbye, dear.
Protect the Spring flowers of
Your beauty. Think of the days
When we were happy together.
If I live I will come back.
If I die, remember me always.

SU WU

Translated by Kenneth Rexroth

WISH FOR A YOUNG WIFE

My lizard, my lively writher,
May your limbs never wither,
May the eyes in your face
Survive the green ice
Of envy's mean gaze;
May you live out your life
Without hate, without grief,
And your hair ever blaze,
In the sun, in the sun,
When I am undone,
When I am no one.

THEODORE ROETHKE

A WEDDING TOAST

M. C. H.
C. H. W.
14 July 1971

St. John tells how, at Cana's wedding-feast,
The water-pots poured wine in such amount
That by his sober count
There were a hundred gallons at the least.

It made no earthly sense, unless to show
How whatsoever love elects to bless
Brims to a sweet excess
That can without depletion overflow.

Which is to say that what love sees is true;
That the world's fullness is not made but found.
Life hungers to abound
And pour its plenty out for such as you.

Now, if your loves will lend an ear to mine,
I toast you both, good son and dear new daughter.
May you not lack for water,
And may that water smack of Cana's wine.

RICHARD WILBUR

PARENT TO CHILD

Lo, children are an heritage of the
LORD: and the fruit of the womb is his
reward.

As arrows are in the hand of a
mighty man; so are children of the
youth.

Happy is the man that hath his
quiver full of them: they shall not be
ashamed, but they shall speak with the
enemies in the gate.

Psalm 127: 3-5

INFANT JOY

"I have no name:
I am but two days old."
What shall I call thee?
"I happy am,
Joy is my name."
Sweet joy befall thee!

Pretty Joy!
Sweet Joy, but two days old.
Sweet Joy I call thee.
Thou dost smile,
I sing the while,
Sweet joy befall thee!

INFANT SORROW

My mother groan'd, my father wept,
Into the dangerous world I leapt;
Helpless, naked, piping loud,
Like a fiend hid in a cloud.

Struggling in my father's hands,
Striving against my swaddling-bands,
Bound and weary, I thought best
To sulk upon my mother's breast.

WILLIAM BLAKE

from ODE: INTIMATIONS OF IMMORTALITY

V

Our birth is but a sleep and a forgetting:
The Soul that rises with us, our life's Star,
    Hath had elsewhere its setting,
      And cometh from afar:
    Not in entire forgetfulness,
    And not in utter nakedness,
But trailing clouds of glory do we come
    From God, who is our home:
Heaven lies about us in our infancy!
Shades of the prison-house begin to close
    Upon the growing Boy,
But He beholds the light, and whence it flows,
    He sees it in his joy;
The Youth, who daily farther from the east
    Must travel, still is Nature's Priest,
    And by the vision splendid
    Is on his way attended;
At length the Man perceives it die away,
And fade into the light of common day.

VI

Earth fills her lap with pleasures of her own;
Yearnings she hath in her own natural kind,
And, even with something of a Mother's mind,
    And no unworthy aim,
    The homely Nurse doth all she can
To make her Foster-child, her Inmate Man,
    Forget the glories he hath known,
And that imperial palace whence he came.

VII

Behold the Child among his new-born blisses,
A six years' Darling of a pigmy size!
See, where 'mid work of his own hand he lies,
Fretted by sallies of his mother's kisses,
With light upon him from his father's eyes!
See, at his feet, some little plan or chart,
Some fragment from his dream of human life,
Shaped by himself with newly-learned art;
    A wedding or a festival,
    A mourning or a funeral;
      And this hath now his heart,
    And unto this he frames his song:
      Then will he fit his tongue
To dialogues of business, love, or strife;
    But it will not be long
    Ere this be thrown aside,
    And with new joy and pride
The little Actor cons another part;
Filling from time to time his "humorous stage"
With all the Persons, down to palsied Age,
That Life brings with her in her equipage;
    As if his whole vocation
    Were endless imitation.

VIII

Thou, whose exterior semblance doth belie
    Thy Soul's immensity;
Thou best Philosopher, who yet dost keep
Thy heritage, thou Eye among the blind,
That, deaf and silent, read'st the eternal deep,
Haunted for ever by the eternal mind, —
    Mighty Prophet! Seer blest!
    On whom those truths do rest,

Which we are toiling all our lives to find,
In darkness lost, the darkness of the grave;
Thou, over whom thy Immortality
Broods like the Day, a Master o'er a Slave,
A Presence which is not to be put by;
Thou little Child, yet glorious in the might
Of heaven-born freedom on thy being's height,
Why with such earnest pains dost thou provoke
The years to bring the inevitable yoke,
Thus blindly with thy blessedness at strife?
Full soon thy Soul shall have her earthly freight,
And custom lie upon thee with a weight,
Heavy as frost, and deep almost as life!

WILLIAM WORDSWORTH

ALL THE LITTLE ANIMALS

"You are not pregnant," said the man
with the probe and the white white coat;
"Yes she is," said all the little animals.
Then the great gynecologist examined. "You are not
    now, and I doubt that you ever have been," he said
    with authority.
"Test me again." He looked at his nurse and shrugged.
"Yes she is," said all the little animals, and laid down
    their lives for my son and me.

Twenty-one years later, my son a grown man and far
    away at the other ocean,
I hear them: "Yes you are," say all the little animals.
I see them, they move in great jumping procession
    through my waking hours,
those frogs and rabbits look at me with their round eyes,
    they kick powerfully with their strong hind legs,
they lay down their lives in silence,
all the rabbits saying Yes, all the frogs saying Yes,
in the face of all men and all institutions,
all the doctors, all the parents, all the worldly friends,
    all the psychiatrists, all the abortionists, all the
    lawyers.
The little animals whom I bless and praise and thank
    forever,
they are part of my living,
go leap through my waking and my sleep, go leap
    through my life and my birth-giving and my death,
go leap through my dreams,
and my son's life
and whatever streams from him.

MURIEL RUKEYSER

43

THE BLESSING OF THE BED

Make the bed
And make the bed,
The sheets are smooth
And the blankets spread.

Back and forth
Round the bed we go,
I and the child
I do not know.

If it shall be
A son I bear,
May he be wise
And kind and fair.

Or if a woman
Child it be,
May the blessings on
Her bed be three.

The first bed
Is the marriage bed:
May Joy and Tenderness
Stand at its head.

And when in childbed
She must lie,
May Victory
Herself draw nigh.

And when at last
Comes the third bed,
May Peace bend down
Above the dead.

Ah, Love! Ennoble
With thy breath
Bride-bed, birth-bed,
And Bed of Death.

Make the bed
And make the bed
The sheets are smooth
And the blankets spread.

ELIZABETH COATSWORTH

MUNDUS ET INFANS

(for Albert and Angelyn Stevens)

Kicking his mother until she let go of his soul
Has given him a healthy appetite: clearly, her rôle
   In the New Order must be
To supply and deliver his raw materials free;
   Should there be any shortage,
She will be held responsible; she also promises
To show him all such attentions as befit his age.
   Having dictated peace,

With one fist clenched behind his head,
   Heel drawn up to thigh
The cocky little ogre dozes off, ready,
   Though, to take on the rest
Of the world at the drop of a hat or the mildest
   Nudge of the impossible,
Resolved, cost what it may, to seize supreme power and
Sworn to resist tyranny to the death with all
   Forces at his command.

A pantheist not a solipsist, he co-operates
With a universe of large and noisy feeling-states
   Without troubling to place
Them anywhere special, for, to his eyes, Funnyface
   Or Elephant as yet
Mean nothing. His distinction between Me and Us
Is a matter of taste; his seasons are Dry and Wet;
   He thinks as his mouth does.

Still, his loud iniquity is still what only the
Greatest of saints become—someone who does not lie:
    He because he cannot
Stop the vivid present to think, they by having got
    Past reflection into
A passionate obedience in time. We have our Boy-
Meets-Girl era of mirrors and muddle to work through,
    Without rest, without joy.

Therefore we love him because his judgments are so
Frankly subjective that his abuse carries no
    Personal sting. We should
Never dare offer our helplessness as a good
    Bargain, without at least
Promising to overcome a misfortune we blame
History or Banks or the Weather for: but this beast
    Dares to exist without shame.

Let him praise our Creator with the top of his voice,
Then, and the motions of his bowels; let us rejoice
    That he lets us hope, for
He may never become a fashionable or
    Important personage:
However bad he may be, he has not yet gone mad;
Whoever we are now, we were no worse at his age;
So of course we ought to be glad

When he bawls the house down. Has he not a perfect
    right
To remind us at every moment how we quite
    Rightly expect each other
To go upstairs or for a walk, if we must cry over
    Spilt milk, such as our wish
That, since apparently we shall never be above
Either or both, we had never learned to distinguish
    Between hunger and love?

                                        W. H. AUDEN

A LEAVE-TAKING

I, who never kissed your head,
Lay these ashes in their bed;
That which I could do have done.
Now farewell, my newborn son.

YVOR WINTERS

METEMPSYCHOSIS

Two months old, already
Across my daughter's face
Pass faces long past and dead.

KENNETH REXROTH

THE GOODNIGHT

He stood still by her bed
Watching his daughter breathe,
The dark and silver head,
The fingers curled beneath,
And thought: Though she may have
Intelligence and charm
And luck, they will not save
Her life from every harm.

The lives of children are
Dangerous to their parents
With fire, water, air,
And other accidents;
And some, for a child's sake,
Anticipating doom,
Empty the world to make
The world safe as a room.

Who could endure the pain
That was Laocoön's?
Twisting, he saw again
In the same coil his sons.
Plumed in his father's skill,
Young Icarus flew higher
Toward the sun, until
He fell in rings of fire.

A man who cannot stand
Children's perilous play,
With lifted voice and hand
Drives the children away.
Out of sight, out of reach,
The tumbling children pass;
He sits on an empty beach,
Holding an empty glass.

Who said that tenderness
Will turn the heart to stone?
May I endure her weakness
As I endure my own.
Better to say goodnight
To breathing flesh and blood
Each night as though the night
Were always only good.

LOUIS SIMPSON

from FROST AT MIDNIGHT

Dear babe, that sleepest cradled by my side,
Whose gentle breathings, heard in this deep calm,
Fill up the interspersèd vacancies
And momentary pauses of the thought!
My babe so beautiful! it thrills my heart
With tender gladness, thus to look at thee,
And think that thou shalt learn far other lore
And in far other scenes! For I was reared
In the great city, pent 'mid cloisters dim,
And saw nought lovely but the sky and stars.
But *thou*, my babe! shalt wander like a breeze
By lakes and sandy shores, beneath the crags
Of ancient mountain, and beneath the clouds,
Which image in their bulk both lakes and shores
And mountain crags: so shalt thou see and hear
The lovely shapes and sounds intelligible
Of that eternal language, which thy God
Utters, who from eternity doth teach
Himself in all, and all things in himself.
Great universal Teacher! He shall mould
Thy Spirit, and by giving make it ask.

Therefore all seasons shall be sweet to thee,
Whether the summer clothe the general earth
With greenness, or the redbreast sit and sing
Betwixt the tufts of snow on the bare branch
Of mossy apple-tree, while the nigh thatch
Smokes in the sun-thaw; whether the eve-drops fall
Heard only in the trances of the blast,
Or if the secret ministry of frost
Shall hang them up in silent icicles,
Quietly shining to the quiet moon.

SAMUEL TAYLOR COLERIDGE

52

THE SONG OF THE OLD MOTHER

I rise in the dawn, and I kneel and blow
Till the seed of the fire flicker and glow;
And then I must scrub and bake and sweep
Till stars are beginning to blink and peep;
And the young lie long and dream in their bed
Of the matching of ribbons for bosom and head,
And their day goes over in idleness,
And they sigh if the wind but lift a tress:
While I must work because I am old,
And the seed of the fire gets feeble and cold.

WILLIAM BUTLER YEATS

THE PARABLE OF
THE PRODIGAL SON

And he said, A certain man had two sons:

And the younger of them said to *his* father, Father, give me the portion of goods that falleth *to me*. And he divided unto them *his* living.

And not many days after the younger son gathered all together, and took his journey into a far country, and there wasted his substance with riotous living.

And when he had spent all, there arose a mighty famine in that land; and he began to be in want.

And he went and joined himself to a citizen of that country; and he sent him into his fields to feed swine.

And he would fain have filled his belly with the husks that the swine did eat: and no man gave unto him.

And when he came to himself, he said, How many hired servants of my father's have bread enough and to spare, and I perish with hunger!

I will arise and go to my father, and will say unto him, Father, I have sinned against heaven, and before thee,

And am no more worthy to be called thy son: make me as one of thy hired servants.

And he arose, and came to his father. But when he was yet a great way off, his father saw him, and had compassion, and ran, and fell on his neck, and kissed him.

And the son said unto him, Father, I have sinned against heaven, and in thy sight, and am no more worthy to be called thy son.

But the father said to his servants, Bring forth the best robe, and put *it* on him; and put a ring on his hand, and shoes on *his* feet:

And bring hither the fatted calf, and kill *it*; and let us eat, and be merry:

For this my son was dead, and is alive again; he was lost, and is found. And they began to be merry.

Now his elder son was in the field: and as he came and drew nigh to the house, he heard music and dancing.

And he called one of the servants, and asked what these things meant.

And he said unto him, Thy brother is come; and thy father hath killed the fatted calf, because he hath received him safe and sound.

And he was angry, and would not go in: therefore came his father out, and entreated him.

And he answering said to *his* father, Lo, these many years do I serve thee, neither transgressed I at any time thy commandment; and yet thou never gavest me a kid, that I might make merry with my friends:

But as soon as this thy son was come, which hath devoured thy living with harlots, thou hast killed for him the fatted calf.

And he said unto him, Son, thou art ever with me, and all that I have is thine.

It was meet that we should make merry, and be glad: for this thy brother was dead, and is alive again; and was lost, and is found.

ST. LUKE 15:11-32

THE PRODIGAL SON

The family gone at last to bed,
He sauntered out to clear his head,
And saw geese hens pears plums hops grain,
His brother's labor through the years.
How blame him that no father's tears
Could keep him from the road again!

THEODORE SPENCER

FOR A CHILD GONE TO LIVE IN A COMMUNE

Outside our ways you found
a way, no name for your home,
no number, not even words.

I thought your voice held onto curves
over cliffs when you said, "We let the animals
have whatever they wanted."

I forgot to tell you: this house too
is a wanderer. Under its paint it is
orbiting all I ever thought it would find—

Those empty spaces. It has found them.

WILLIAM STAFFORD

THE BOOK
—for Richard Howard

You, hiding there in your words
like a disgrace
the cast-off son of a family
whose face is written in theirs
who must not be mentioned
who calls collect three times a year
from obscure towns out-of-state
and whose calls are never accepted
You who had to leave alone
and forgot your shadow hanging under the stairs
let me tell you: I have been in the house
I have spoken to all of them
they will not pronounce your name
they only allude to you
rising and sitting, going or coming,
falling asleep and waking,
giving away in marriage or calling for water
on their deathbeds
their faces look into each other and see
you
when they write at night in their diaries they are writing
to you

ADRIENNE RICH

from *HENRY IV: PART I*

KING.

Yea, there thou makest me sad and makest me sin
In envy that my Lord Northumberland
Should be the father to so blest a son,
A son who is the theme of honor's tongue;
Amongst a grove, the very straightest plant;
Who is sweet Fortune's minion and her pride:
Whilst I, by looking on the praise of him,
See riot and dishonor stain the brow
Of my young Harry. O that it could be proved
That some night-tripping fairy had exchanged
In cradle-clothes our children where they lay,
And call'd mine Percy, his Plantagenet!
Then would I have his Harry, and he mine.

WILLIAM SHAKESPEARE

DAVID AND ABSALOM

And David sat between the two gates: and the watchman went up to the roof over the gate unto the wall, and lifted up his eyes, and looked, and behold a man running alone.

And the watchman cried, and told the king. And the king said, If he be alone, there is tidings in his mouth. And he came apace, and drew near.

And the watchman saw another man running: and the watchman called unto the porter, and said, Behold another man running alone. And the king said, He also bringeth tidings.

And the watchman said, Me thinketh the running of the foremost is like the running of Ahimaaz the son of Zadok. And the king said, He is a good man, and cometh with good tidings.

And Ahimaaz called, and said unto the king, All is well. And he fell down to the earth upon his face before the king, and said, Blessed be the Lord thy God, which hath delivered up the men that lifted up their hand against my lord the king.

And the king said, Is the young man Absalom safe? And Ahimaaz answered, When Joab sent the king's servant, and me thy servant, I saw a great tumult, but I knew not what it was.

And the king said unto him, Turn aside, and stand here. And he turned aside, and stood still.

And, behold, Cushi came; and Cushi said, Tidings, my lord the king: for the Lord hath avenged thee this day of all them that rose up against thee.

And the king said unto Cushi, Is the young man Absalom safe? And Cushi answered, The enemies of my lord the king, and all that rise against thee to do thee hurt, be as that young man is.

And the king was much moved, and went up to the chamber over the gate, and wept: and as he went, thus he said, O my son Absalom, my son, my son Absalom! would God I had died for thee, O Absalom, my son, my son!

II SAMUEL 18:24-33

RANDALL, MY SON

Randall, my son, before you came just now
I saw the lean vine fingering at the latch,
And through the rain I heard the poplar bough
Thresh at the blinds it never used to touch,
And I was old and troubled overmuch,
And called in the deep night, but there was none
To comfort me or answer, Randall, my son.

But mount the stair and lay you down till morn.
The bed is made—the lamp is burning low.
Within the changeless room where you were born
I wait the changing day when you must go.
I am unreconciled to what I know,
And I am old with questions never done
That will not let me slumber, Randall, my son.

Randall, my son, I cannot hear the cries
That lure beyond familiar fields, or see
The glitter of the world that draws your eyes.
Cold is the mistress that beckons you from me.
I wish her sleek hunting might never come to be—
For in our woods where deer and fox still run
An old horn blows at daybreak, Randall, my son.

And tell me then, will you some day bequeath
To your own son not born or yet begotten,
The luster of a sword that sticks in sheath,
A house that crumbles and a fence that's rotten?
Take, what I leave, your own land unforgotten;
Hear, what I hear, in a far chase new begun
An old horn's husky music, Randall, my son.

DONALD DAVIDSON

GODCHILDREN

Children of mine, not mine but lent
By generous parents, what sweet grief
I take from our clumsy make-belief,
Neither fulfilled nor discontent.

From my mock-parenthood I learn
Domestic uses, while you feed
Promiscuously in your need
For love, and all love serves your turn.

The bond I gave to set you free
In childhood was my soul in prayer.
I had not thought to bargain there
But you stand sponsors now for me.

My fantasy is this: alone,
Like orphans in reverse, are whirled
The seedless god-folk of the world
And then redeemed by this bright loan.

                              WILLIAM MEREDITH

from *HEART'S NEEDLE*

1

Child of my winter, born
When the new fallen soldiers froze
In Asia's steep ravines and fouled the snows,
When I was torn

By love I could not still,
By fear that silenced my cramped mind
To that cold war where, lost, I could not find
My peace in my will,

All those days we could keep
Your mind a landscape of new snow
Where the chilled tenant-farmer finds, below,
His fields asleep

In their smooth covering, white
As quilts to warm the resting bed
Of birth or pain, spotless as paper spread
For me to write,

And thinks: Here lies my land
Unmarked by agony, the lean foot
Of the weasel tracking, the thick trapper's boot;
And I have planned

My chances to restrain
The torments of demented summer or
Increase the deepening harvest here before
It snows again.

2

Late April and you are three; today
   We dug your garden in the yard.
To curb the damage of your play,
Strange dogs at night and the moles tunneling,
   Four slender sticks of lath stand guard
      Uplifting their thin string.

So you were the first to tramp it down.
   And after the earth was sifted close
You brought your watering can to drown
All earth *and* us. But these mixed seeds are pressed
   With light loam in their steadfast rows.
      Child, we've done our best.

Someone will have to weed and spread
   The young sprouts. Sprinkle them in the hour
When shadow falls across their bed.
You should try to look at them every day
   Because when they come to full flower
      I will be away.

W. D. SNODGRASS

TO MY DAUGHTER

Bright clasp of her whole hand around my finger,
My daughter, as we walk together now.
All my life I'll feel a ring invisibly
Circle this bone with shining: when she is grown
Far from today as her eyes are far already.

STEPHEN SPENDER

LINES TO THREE BOYS,
8, 6-1/2, AND 2 YEARS OF AGE

Gentlemen, I love and like you,
Caring little for your IQ.

F.P.A.

THE CORNFIELD

Up to the cornfield, old and curly,
I took Joe, who rises early.
Joe my yearling, on my shoulder,
Observed the old corn growing older.
And I could feel the simple awe
He felt at seeing what he saw:
Yellow light and cool day
And cornstalks stretching far away.
My son, too young and wise to speak,
Clung with one hand to my cheek,
While in his head were slowly born
Important mysteries of the corn.
And being present at the birth
Of my child's wonderment at earth,
I felt my own life stir again
By the still graveyard of the grain.

E. B. WHITE

COMPLICATED THOUGHTS
ABOUT A SMALL SON

In you, in you I see myself,
  Or what I like to think is me;
You are the man, the little man
  I've never had the time to be.

In you I read the crystal line
  I'll never get around to writing;
In you I taste the only wine
  That makes the world at all exciting.

And that, to give you breath and blood
  Was trick beyond my simple scope,
Is everything I know of good
  And everything I see of hope.

And since, to write in blood and breath
  Was fairer than my fairest dream,
The manuscript I leave for death
  Is you, whose life supplied its theme.

E. B. WHITE

LYRIC FOR THE FATHER
OF A GIRL

The child that came a stranger from
A cold, troubled ocean—born
Flushed as a sea robin, wild as a sea lily—

Touched me like morning; as from sleep,
I followed her, perplexed, to her dominion,
Marine and violet, this somewhere cold and sure

I could not go without her. Here I tried to teach her.
By my small parent precision, taught her names:
Learning at last my language, she told me the hours.

Her feet unlocked doors, windows, hidden ways,
Mines at her touch spilled wide as shells;
She knew this. It was hers.

Sand shifted through her listening fingers as she
Walked crab-backwards in the salt sun. I heard.
Seals, just beyond us, barked and glittered.

Surrendering her, I found I had nowhere to go.
She called to me and stared. By my dry tongue,
She learned in words that I had taught her

Fear that made me strange to her. I told her,
Sunday I'll come always, but the sea grew small,
The shore turned black, and the tide flew out in a torrent.

V. R. LANG

THROUGH THE VINES

for our son

Before I fed
upon the olive,
bitter curd
was my food,

a motley mantle
patched my naked-
ness and nude
word in winters
of the will,

no seraph waited
at the threshold
of my sleep,
of my vigil.

Then need was seed.
Your branches bore
an ardor weightless,
winged. I wore
the suit of seemliness.

With the early leaves
that, restless,
fall to flame,
your limbs were blessed.

Through the vines,
a seraph laughs.

ALLEN MANDELBAUM

BROTHERS & SISTERS

Behold, how good and how pleasant
it is for brethren to dwell together
in unity!

Psalm 133:1

CAIN AND ABEL

And Adam knew Eve his wife; and she conceived, and bare Cain, and said, I have gotten a man from the Lord.

And she again bare his brother Abel. And Abel was a keeper of sheep, but Cain was a tiller of the ground.

And in process of time it came to pass, that Cain brought of the fruit of the ground an offering unto the Lord.

And Abel, he also brought of the firstlings of his flock and of the fat thereof. And the Lord had respect unto Abel and to his offering:

But unto Cain and to his offering he had not respect. And Cain was very wroth, and his countenance fell.

And the Lord said unto Cain, Why art thou wroth? and why is thy countenance fallen?

If thou doest well, shalt thou not be accepted? and if thou doest not well, sin lieth at the door. And unto thee shall be his desire, and thou shalt rule over him.

And Cain talked with Abel his brother: and it came to pass, when they were in the field, that Cain rose up against Abel his brother, and slew him.

And the Lord said unto Cain, Where is Abel thy brother? And he said, I know not: Am I my brother's keeper?

And he said, What hast thou done? the voice of thy brother's blood crieth unto me from the ground.

And now art thou cursed from the earth, which hath opened her mouth to receive thy brother's blood from thy hand;

When thou tillest the ground, it shall not henceforth yield unto thee her strength; a fugitive and a vagabond shalt thou be in the earth.

And Cain said unto the Lord, My punishment is greater than I can bear.

Behold, thou hast driven me out this day from the face of the earth; and from thy face shall I be hid; and I shall be a fugitive and a vagabond in the earth; and it shall come to pass, that every one that findeth me shall slay me.

And the Lord said unto him, Therefore whosoever slayeth Cain, vengeance shall be taken on him sevenfold. And the Lord set a mark upon Cain, lest any finding him should kill him.

GENESIS 4:1-15

CAIN

the land of Nod
is a desert
on my head   I
plant tears
every morning,
my brother
don't rise up

LUCILLE CLIFTON

TO MY BROTHERS

Small, busy flames play through the fresh laid coals,
 And their faint cracklings o'er our silence creep
 Like whispers of the household gods that keep
A gentle empire o'er fraternal souls.
And while, for rhymes, I search around the poles,
 Your eyes are fix'd, as in poetic sleep,
 Upon the lore so voluble and deep,
That aye at fall of night our care condoles.
This is your birth-day Tom, and I rejoice
 That thus it passes smoothly, quietly.
Many such eves of gently whisp'ring noise
 May we together pass, and calmly try
What are this world's true joys,—ere the great voice,
 From its fair face, shall bid our spirits fly.

JOHN KEATS

CARL

Like a great tree
Spread over me,
With love in every limb:
I worshipped him.

MARK VAN DOREN

THE BROTHERS

Last night I watched my brothers play,
The gentle and the reckless one,
In a field two yards away.
For half a century they were gone
Beyond the other side of care
To be among the peaceful dead.
Even in a dream how could I dare
Interrogate that happiness
So wildly spent yet never less?
For still they raced about the green
And were like two revolving suns;
A brightness poured from head to head,
So strong I could not see their eyes
Or look into their paradise.
What were they doing, the happy ones?
Yet where I was they once had been.

I thought, How could I be so dull,
Twenty thousand days ago,
Not to see they were beautiful?
I asked them, Were you really so
As you are now, that other day?
And the dream was soon away.

For then we played for victory
And not to make each other glad.
A darkness covered every head,
Frowns twisted the original face,
And through that mask we could not see
The beauty and the buried grace.

I have observed in foolish awe
The dateless mid-days of the law
And seen indifferent justice done
By everyone on everyone.
And in a vision I have seen
My brothers playing on the green.

EDWIN MUIR

TO MY BROTHER

Killed: Haumont Wood: October, 1918

O you so long dead,
You masked and obscure,
I can tell you, all things endure:
The wine and the bread;

The marble quarried for the arch;
The iron become steel;
The spoke broken from the wheel;
The sweat of the long march;

The hay-stacks cut through like loaves
And the hundred flowers from the seed;
All things indeed
Though struck by the hooves

Of disaster, of time due,
Of fell loss and gain,
All things remain,
I can tell you, this is true.

Though burned down to stone
Though lost from the eye,
I can tell you, and not lie,—
Save of peace alone.

LOUISE BOGAN

TO HIS BROTHER HSING-CHIEN

(A.D. 820)

Can the single cup of wine
We drank this morning have made my heart so glad?
This is a joy that comes only from within,
Which those who witness will never understand.
   I have but two brothers
And bitterly grieved that both were far away;
This Spring, back through the Gorges of Pa,
I have come to them safely, ten thousand leagues.
   Two sisters I had
Who had put up their hair, but not twined the sash;*
Yesterday both were married and taken away
By good husbands in whom I may well trust.
I am freed at last from the thoughts that made me grieve,
As though a sword had cut a rope from my neck.
And limbs grow light when the heart sheds its care:
Suddenly I seem to be flying up to the sky!

Hsing-chien, drink your cup of wine
Then set it down and listen to what I say.
Do not sigh that your home is far away;
Do not mind if your salary is small.
Only pray that as long as life lasts,
You and I may never be forced to part.

PO CHU-I
Translated by Arthur Waley

---

* *I.e.,* got married

TO HIS BROTHER DEAD

CI—Multas per gentes et
multa per aequora vectus

By ways remote and distant waters sped,
    Brother, to thy sad graveside am I come,
That I may give the last gifts to the dead
    And vainly parley with thine ashes dumb;
Since she who now bestows and now denies
    Hath ta'en thee, hapless brother, from mine eyes.
But lo! these gifts, the heirlooms of past years,
    Are made sad things to grace thy coffin-shell;
Take them, all drenchèd with a brother's tears,
    And, brother, for all time, hail and farewell.

CATULLUS

Translated by Aubrey Beardsley

ADAPTATION OF A THEME BY CATULLUS

(From the translation by Aubrey Beardsley)

Carmen CI
Past towns, states, deserts, hills and rivers borne
By the first plane, brother, I've come today,
A spirit, to linger at your spiritless clay
That sleeps well-dressed beyond the reach of scorn:
Not glad, lifeless tycoon, nor sorry feel
For neither Bull nor Bear attends your way—
Ah, vanity of speech, what should I say?
The grave encloses you with technical zeal
For Chance, swift giver, may just as swiftly take.
Accept these costly wreaths for my own sake
(Death asks no entrance fee to let you in)
And for the decent sense of heaven and hell:
Take them, and think not much on mortal sin.
Now, brother, time being money, I say farewell.

ALLEN TATE

IN THE TREE HOUSE AT NIGHT

And now the green household is dark.
The half-moon completely is shining
On the earth-lighted tops of the trees.
To be dead, a house must be still.
The floor and the walls wave me slowly;
I am deep in them over my head.
The needles and pine cones about me

Are full of small birds at their roundest,
Their fists without mercy gripping
Hard down through the tree to the roots
To sing back at light when they feel it.
We lie here like angels in bodies,
My brothers and I, one dead,
The other asleep from much living,

In mid-air huddled beside me.
Dark climbed to us here as we climbed
Up the nails I have hammered all day
Through the sprained, comic rungs of the ladder
Of broom handles, crate slats, and laths
Foot by foot up the trunk to the branches
Where we came out at last over lakes

Of leaves, of fields disencumbered of earth
That move with the moves of the spirit.
Each nail that sustains us I set here;
Each nail in the house is now steadied
By my dead brother's huge, freckled hand.
Through the years, he has pointed his hammer
Up into these limbs, and told us

That we must ascend, and all lie here.
Step after step he has brought me,
Embracing the trunk as his body,
Shaking its limbs with my heartbeat,
Till the pine cones danced without wind
And fell from the branches like apples.
In the arm-slender forks of our dwelling

I breathe my live brother's light hair.
The blanket around us becomes
As solid as stone, and it sways.
With all my heart, I close
The blue, timeless eye of my mind.
Wind springs, as my dead brother smiles
And touches the tree at the root;

A shudder of joy runs up
The trunk; the needles tingle;
One bird uncontrollably cries.
The wind changes round, and I stir
Within another's life. Whose life?
Who is dead? Whose presence is living?
When may I fall strangely to earth,

Who am nailed to this branch by a spirit?
Can two bodies make up a third?
To sing, must I feel the world's light?
My green, graceful bones fill the air
With sleeping birds. Alone, alone
And with them I move gently.
I move at the heart of the world.

JAMES DICKEY

THE TWINS

Likeness has made them animal and shy.
See how they turn their full gaze left and right,
Seeking the other, yet not moving close;
Nothing in their relationship is gross,
But soft, conspicuous, like giraffes. And why
Do they not speak except by sudden sight?

Sisters kiss freely and unsubtle friends
Wrestle like lovers; brothers loudly laugh:
These in a dreamier bondage dare not touch.
Each is the other's soul and hears too much
The heartbeat of the other; each apprehends
The sad duality and the imperfect half.

The one lay sick, the other wandered free,
But like a child to a small plot confined
Walked a short way and dumbly reappeared.
Is it not all-in-all of what they feared,
The single death, the obvious destiny
That maims the miracle their will designed?

For they go emptily from face to face,
Keeping the instinctive partnership of birth
A ponderous marriage and a sacred name;
Theirs is the pride of shouldering each the same
The old indignity of Esau's* race
And Dromio's* denouement of tragic mirth.

KARL SHAPIRO

---

*Esau was the twin of Jacob; Dromio of Ephesus was the twin of
Dromio of Syracuse, in Shakespeare's *Comedy of Errors*.

from *LINES COMPOSED A FEW MILES ABOVE TINTERN ABBEY*

For thou art with me here upon the banks
Of this fair river; thou my dearest Friend,
My dear, dear Friend; and in thy voice I catch
The language of my former heart, and read
My former pleasures in the shooting lights
Of thy wild eyes. Oh! yet a little while
May I behold in thee what I was once,
My dear, dear Sister! and this prayer I make,
Knowing that Nature never did betray
The heart that loved her; 'tis her privilege,
Through all the years of this our life, to lead
From joy to joy: for she can so inform
The mind that is within us, so impress
With quietness and beauty, and so feed
With lofty thoughts, that neither evil tongues,
Rash judgments, nor the sneers of selfish men,
Nor greetings where no kindness is, nor all
The dreary intercourse of daily life,
Shall e'er prevail against us, or disturb
Our cheerful faith, that all which we behold
Is full of blessings. Therefore let the moon
Shine on thee in thy solitary walk;
And let the misty mountain-winds be free
To blow against thee: and, in after years,
When these wild ecstasies shall be matured
Into a sober pleasure; when thy mind
Shall be a mansion for all lovely forms,
Thy memory be as a dwelling-place
For all sweet sounds and harmonies; oh! then,

If solitude, or fear, or pain, or grief,
Should be thy portion, with what healing thoughts
Of tender joy wilt thou remember me,
And these my exhortations! Nor, perchance—
If I should be where I no more can hear
Thy voice, nor catch from thy wild eyes these gleams
Of past existence—wilt thou then forget
That on the banks of this delightful stream
We stood together; and that I, so long
A worshipper of Nature, hither came
Unwearied in that service: rather say
With warmer love—oh! with far deeper zeal
Of holier love. Nor wilt thou then forget,
That after many wanderings, many years
Of absence, these steep woods and lofty cliffs,
And this green pastoral landscape, were to me
More dear, both for themselves and for thy sake!

WILLIAM WORDSWORTH

WINTER VERSE FOR HIS SISTER

Moonlight washes the west side of the house
As clean as bone, it carpets like a lawn
The stubbled field tilting eastward
Where there is no sign yet of dawn.
The moon is an angel with a bright light sent
To surprise me once before I die
With the real aspect of things.
It holds the light steady and makes no comment.

Practicing for death I have lately gone
To that other house
Where our parents did most of their dying,
Embracing and not embracing their conditions.
Our father built bookcases and little by little stopped
    reading,
Our mother cooked proud meals for common mouths.
Kindly, they raised two children. We raked their leaves
And cut their grass, we ate and drank with them.
Reconciliation was our long work, not all of it joyful.

Now outside my own house at a cold hour
I watch the noncommittal angel lower
The steady lantern that's worn these clapboards thin
In a wash of moonlight, while men slept within,
Accepting and not accepting their conditions,
And the fingers of trees plied a deep carpet of decay
On the gravel web underneath the field,
And the field tilting always toward day.

WILLIAM MEREDITH

91

ANCESTORS & DESCENDANTS

For enquire, I pray thee, of the
former age, and prepare thyself to
the search of their fathers.

Job 8:8

THE MOTHER

On the hilltop, close to the house of the empress,
    Your temple
Is dark, sunken: a pit. The thick crowded pillars
Stumps only. The dread of Your presence
Lopped, like them, cold in mutilation.
Throning it here, in the stillness: vacancy.
In times beyond this time, were you robed in darkness?
You were known, then, as the Great Goddess. You are
Great even yet, more terrible, Mother Cybele, now you
    are nothing.

BABETTE DEUTSCH

THE IRISH CLIFFS OF MOHER

Who is my father in this world, in this house,
At the spirit's base?

My father's father, his father's father, his—
Shadows like winds

Go back to a parent before thought, before speech,
At the head of the past.

They go to the cliffs of Moher rising out of the mist,
Above the real,

Rising out of present time and place, above
The wet, green grass.

This is not landscape, full of the somnambulations
Of poetry

And the sea. This is my father or, maybe,
It is as he was,

A likeness, one of the race of fathers: earth
And sea and air.

WALLACE STEVENS

HEREDITY

I am the family face;
Flesh perishes, I live on,
Projecting trait and trace
Through time to times anon,
And leaping from place to place
Over oblivion.

The years-heired feature that can
In curve and voice and eye
Despise the human span
Of durance—that is I;
The eternal thing in man,
That heeds no call to die.

THOMAS HARDY

ANCESTORS

The child enquires about his ancestors
    And looks from one stem to the other.
His questions make me gaze beyond the now
That trembles in the frailty of his mother.

And more: behind my self, compact, I see
    Irrelevant creatures of the past –
Giants of childhood, portraits on the wall,
Those of whom once I thought I was the last.

This bone-hard flesh I feel, the mind I use,
    Stretch over ages like a trope,
And face and feeling die and reappear
Till time has worn them perfect for my scope.

What I am like's an island, gnawed and drenched,
    Whose long root through the flux preserves;
With nose as dreaded, steered-for promontory,
And culture hanging on its mineral nerves.

So to the boy this haunted shade replies:
    Your ancestors were like you but grotesque:
Few are remembered, though to make you all
Feared for their sons, wrote verses at a desk.

ROY FULLER

"The child is father to the man."
How can he be? The words are wild.
Suck any sense from that who can:
"The child is father to the man."
No; what the poet did write ran,
"The man is father to the child."
"The child is father to the man!"
How *can* he be? The words are wild.

GERARD MANLEY HOPKINS

"The child is father of the man"—William Wordsworth

≥ *99*

from LETTER TO LORD BYRON

My father's forbears were all Midland yeomen
   Till royalties from coal mines did them good;
I think they must have been phlegmatic slowmen.
   My mother's ancestors had Norman blood.
   From Somerset I've always understood;
My grandfathers on either side agree
In being clergymen and C. of E.

Father and Mother each was one of seven,
   Though one died young and one was not all there;
Their fathers both went suddenly to Heaven
   While they were still quite small and left them here
   To work on earth with little cash to spare;
A nurse, a rising medico, at Bart's
Both felt the pangs of Cupid's naughty darts.

My home then was professional and 'high'.
   No gentler father ever lived, I'll lay
All Lombard Street against a shepherd's pie.
   We imitate our loves: well, neighbours say
   I grow more like my mother every day.
I don't like business men. I know a Prot
Will never really kneel, but only squat.

In pleasures of the mind they both delighted;
   The library in the study was enough
To make a better boy than me short-sighted;
   Our old cook Ada surely knew her stuff;
   My elder brothers did not treat me rough;
We lived at Solihull, a village then;
Those at the gasworks were my favourite men.

My earliest recollection to stay put
   Is of a white stone doorstep and a spot
Of pus where father lanced the terrier's foot;
   Next, stuffing shag into the coffee pot
   Which nearly killed my mother, but did not;
Both psychoanalyst and Christian minister
Will think these incidents extremely sinister.

W. H. AUDEN

A HOUSEHOLD

When, to disarm suspicious minds at lunch
Before coming to the point, or at golf,
The bargain driven, to soothe hurt feelings,

He talks about his home, he never speaks
(A reticence for which they all admire him)
Of his bride so worshipped and so early lost,

But proudly tells of that young scamp his heir,
Of black eyes given and received, thrashings
Endured without a sound to save a chum;

Or calls their spotted maleness to revere
His saintly mother, calm and kind and wise,
A grand old lady pouring out the tea.

Whom, though, has he ever asked for the week-end?
Out to his country mansion in the evening,
Another merger signed, he drives alone:

To be avoided by a miserable runt
Who wets his bed and cannot throw or whistle,
A tell-tale, a crybaby, a failure;

To the revilings of a slatternly hag
Who caches bottles in her mattress, spits
And shouts obscenities from the landing;

Worse, to find both in an unholy alliance,
Youth stealing Age the liquor-cupboard key,
Age teaching Youth to lie with a straight face.

Disgraces to keep hidden from the world
Where rivals, envying his energy and brains
And with rattling skeletons of their own,

Would see in him the villain of this household,
Whose bull-voice scared a sensitive young child,
Whose coldness drove a doting parent mad.

Besides (which might explain why he has neither
Altered his will nor called the doctor in),
He half believes, call it a superstition,

It is for his sake that they hate and fear him:
Should they unmask and show themselves worth loving,
Loving and sane and manly, he would die.

W. H. AUDEN

SCENE FROM THE WORKING CLASS
To Richard Hoggart*

Two nasty little houses back to back.
The single room smelling of sister's face
powder and father's tripe-and-onion stew,
the coin box full of pennies on the shelf
and all a family's future held in place.
Each week was like each week. This was your self
and father come in late from mill or mine
and Mondays mother hung the washing on the line.
Sunday sacred to the last generation,
uncle and aunt, grandparents coming in
to tea. You always opened up a tin
of pineapple and one of salmon. Celebration.
Two nasty little houses back to back,
and one held you and all your family,
your coal fire company savings love and heat,
your girl and future wife from down the street,
and when the poker banged against the grate
behind the wall, it meant a heart attack
or baby's coming, and you could not wait.

                                   RICHMOND LATTIMORE

---

*Author of *Speaking to Each Other: Aspects of Working-Class Life*
—H.P.

THE FAMILY DINNER-PARTY

What a thing to come upon relations sitting at their food!
Father first will take the cup and tell you something for
    your good,
Washing down a heavy humour. Mother then must do
    her bit;
Next a nurse chips in with comment; a deep rumble
    seconds it,
—That is grand-pa. Then some grannie calls the lad a
    "pet"; and he
Nods assent to every speaker, too polite to disagree.

MENANDER
Translated by C. M. Bowra

MY MOTHER'S SISTER

I see her against the pearl sky of Dublin
Before the turn of the century, a young woman
With all those brothers and sisters, green eyes, hair
She could sit on; for high life, a meandering sermon

(Church of Ireland) each Sunday, window-shopping
In Dawson Street, picnics at Killiney and Howth . . .
To know so little about the growing of one
Who was angel and maid-of-all-work to my growth!

—Who, her sister dying, took on the four-year
Child, and the chance that now she would never make
A child of her own; who, mothering me, flowered in
The clover-soft authority of the meek.

Who, exiled, gossiping home chat from abroad
In roundhand letters to a drift of relations—
Squires', Goldsmiths, Overends, Williams'—sang
        the songs
Of Zion in a strange land. Hers the patience

Of one who made no claims, but simply loved
Because that was her nature, and loving so
Asked no more than to be repaid in kind.
If she was not a saint, I do not know

What saints are . . . Buying penny toys at Christmas
(The most a small purse could afford) to send her
Nephews and nieces, she'd never have thought the shop
Could shine for me one day in Bethlehem splendour.

Exiled again after ten years, my father
Remarrying, she faced the bitter test
Of charity—to abdicate in love's name
From love's contentful duties. A distressed

Gentle woman housekeeping for strangers;
Later, companion to a droll recluse
Clergyman brother in rough-pastured Wexford,
She lived for all she was worth—to be of use.

She bottled plums, she visited parishioners.
A plain habit of innocence, a faith
Mildly forbearing, made her one of those
Who, we were promised, shall inherit the earth.

. . . Now, sunk in one small room of a Rathmines
Old people's home, helpless, beyond speech
Or movement, yearly deeper she declines
To imbecility—my last link with childhood.

The battery's almost done: yet if I press
The button hard—some private joke in boyhood
I teased her with—there comes upon her face
A glowing of the old, enchanted smile.

So, still alive, she rots. A heart of granite
Would melt at this unmeaning sequel. Lord,
How can this be justified, how can it
Be justified?

C. DAY LEWIS

TO AUNTIE

Chief of our aunts—not only I,
But all your dozen of nurslings cry—
What did the other children do?
And what were childhood, wanting you?

ROBERT LOUIS STEVENSON

THE NIECE AT THE DEATHBED

A world of cocoa, silk, and cards,
And of old age the loneliness,
Of checks for Christmas and rewards
Shrunk down to praise of a new dress,
I watch, I watch, and cannot cry
More with my tears than "This is I."

THEODORE SPENCER

ELEGY

Her face like a rain-beaten stone on the day she
        rolled off
With the dark hearse, and enough flowers for an
        alderman,—
And so she was, in her way, Aunt Tilly.

Sighs, sighs, who says they have sequence?
Between the spirit and the flesh,—what war?
She never knew;
For she asked no quarter and gave none,
Who sat with the dead when the relatives left,
Who fed and tended the infirm, the mad, the epileptic,
And, with a harsh rasp of a laugh at herself,
Faced up to the worst.

I recall how she harried the children away all the late
        summer
From the one beautiful thing in her yard, the peachtree;
How she kept the wizened, the fallen, the misshapen
        for herself,
And picked and pickled the best, to be left on rickety
        doorsteps.

And yet she died in agony,
Her tongue, at the last, thick, black as an ox's.

Terror of cops, bill collectors, betrayers of the poor,—
I see you in some celestial supermarket,
Moving serenely among the leeks and cabbages,
Probing the squash,
Bearing down, with two steady eyes,
On the quaking butcher.

THEODORE ROETHKE

110

NEW ENGLAND PROTESTANT

When Aunt Emily died, her husband would not look
    at her.
Uncle Peter, inarticulate in his cold intelligence,
Conceded few flowers, arranged the simplest service.
Only the intimate members of the family came.

Then the small procession went to the family grave.
No word was spoken but the parson's solemn few.
Silence, order, a prim dryness, not a tear.
We left the old man standing alone there.

RICHARD EBERHART

MY UNCLE

I think of forests palaces and swans
and Chinese painted scrolls and figured silk,
breakfasts of wine-and-tapioca soup,

of limericks and psalms, jade rings and beer,
of mad King Ludwig on his porcelain eggs,
a baroque cardinal or the knave of clubs.

An elder. So much younger when he died
than I am now. Blood bursting in the head.
Florence, which he loved best who holds him now.

Once slim, they tell me, so poetical.
I knew a leisured height, a handsome head,
bold nose, a ripe mouth, and fastidious hands.

He would amuse spoiled children. Catholic
spellbound childlike in ceremony. What
hard faith stuck underneath, this puzzles me.

His mind as a cathedral arched and domed.
Musing imagination flew such form
as could not think to lose all opulence.

Rococo is the word. A glory grew
exotic to its circumstance, so loved,
smiled on, encouraged, and misunderstood.

Dreamy my uncle drifts on pinkish clouds.
His heaven or my hope, how shall I know?
His cherubs would sing well. I hope they do.

RICHMOND LATTIMORE

DEAD BOY

The little cousin is dead, by foul subtraction,
A green bough from Virginia's aged tree,
And none of the county kin like the transaction,
Nor some of the world of outer dark, like me.

A boy not beautiful, nor good, nor clever,
A black cloud full of storms too hot for keeping,
A sword beneath his mother's heart—yet never
Woman bewept her babe as this is weeping.

A pig with a pasty face, so I had said,
Squealing for cookies, kinned by poor pretense
With a noble house. But the little man quite dead,
I see the forbears' antique lineaments.

The elder men have strode by the box of death
To the wide flag porch, and muttering low send round
The bruit of the day. O friendly waste of breath!
Their hearts are hurt with a deep dynastic wound.

He was pale and little, the foolish neighbors say;
The first-fruits, saith the Preacher, the Lord hath taken;
But this was the old tree's late branch wrenched away,
Grieving the sapless limbs, the shorn and shaken.

JOHN CROWE RANSOM

Children's children are the crown of old men;
and the glory of children are their fathers.

OLD MAN PLAYING WITH CHILDREN

A discreet householder exclaims on the grandsire
In warpaint and feathers, with fierce grandsons and axes
Dancing round a backyard fire of boxes:
"Watch grandfather, he'll set the house on fire."

But I will unriddle for you the thought of his mind,
An old one you cannot open with conversation.
What animates the thin legs in risky motion?
Mixes the snow on the head with snow on the wind?

"Grandson, grandsire. We are equally boy and boy.
Do not offer your reclining-chair and slippers
With tedious old women talking in wrappers.
This life is not good but in danger and in joy.

"It is you the elder to these and younger to me
Who are penned as slaves by properties and causes
And never walk from your insupportable houses
And shamefully, when boys shout, go in and flee.

"May God forgive me, I know your middling ways,
Having taken care and performed ignominies unreckoned
Between the first brief childhood and the brief second,
But I will be more honorable in these days."

JOHN CROWE RANSOM

MANNERS

for a Child of 1918

My grandfather said to me
as we sat on the wagon seat,
"Be sure to remember to always
speak to everyone you meet."

We met a stranger on foot.
My grandfather's whip tapped his hat.
"Good day, sir. Good day. A fine day."
And I said it and bowed where I sat.

Then we overtook a boy we knew
with his big pet crow on his shoulder.
"Always offer everyone a ride;
don't forget that when you get older,"

my grandfather said. So Willy
climbed up with us, but the crow
gave a "Caw!" and flew off. I was worried.
How would he know where to go?

But he flew a little way at a time
from fence post to fence post, ahead;
and when Willy whistled he answered.
"A fine bird," my grandfather said,

"and he's well brought up. See, he answers
nicely when he's spoken to.
Man or beast, that's good manners.
Be sure that you both always do."

When automobiles went by,
the dust hid the people's faces,
but we shouted "Good day! Good day!
Fine day!" at the top of our voices.

When we came to Hustler Hill,
he said that the mare was tired,
so we all got down and walked,
as our good manners required.

ELIZABETH BISHOP

SIRE

Here comes the shadow not looking where it is going,
And the whole night will fall; it is time.
Here comes the little wind which the hour
Drags with it everywhere like an empty wagon
    through leaves.
Here comes my ignorance shuffling after them
Asking them what they are doing.

Standing still, I can hear my footsteps
Come up behind me and go on
Ahead of me and come up behind me and
With different keys clinking in the pockets,
And still I do not move. Here comes
The white-haired thistle seed stumbling past through
    the branches
Like a paper lantern carried by a blind man.
I believe it is the lost wisdom of my grandfather
Whose ways were his own and who died before I
    could ask.

Forerunner, I would like to say, silent pilot,
Little dry death, future,
Your indirections are as strange to me
As my own. I know so little that anything
You might tell me would be a revelation.

Sir, I would like to say,
It is hard to think of the good woman
Presenting you with children, like cakes,
Granting you the eye of her needle,
Standing in doorways, flinging after you
Little endearments, like rocks, or her silence
Like a whole Sunday of bells. Instead, tell me:

Which of my many incomprehensions
Did you bequeath me, and where did they take you?
    Standing
In the shoes of indecision, I hear them
Come up behind me and go on ahead of me
Wearing boots, on crutches, barefoot, they could never
Get together on any door-sill or destination—
The one with the assortment of smiles, the one
Jailed in himself like a forest, the one who comes
Back at evening drunk with despair and turns
Into the wrong night as though he owned it—oh small
Deaf disappearance in the dusk, in which of their shoes
Will I find myself tomorrow?

W. S. MERWIN

SESTINA

September rain falls on the house.
In the failing light, the old grandmother
sits in the kitchen with the child
beside the Little Marvel Stove,
reading the jokes from the almanac,
laughing and talking to hide her tears.

She thinks that her equinoctial tears
and the rain that beats on the roof of the house
were both foretold by the almanac,
but only known to a grandmother.
The iron kettle sings on the stove.
She cuts some bread and says to the child,

It's time for tea now; but the child
is watching the teakettle's small hard tears
dance like mad on the hot black stove,
the way the rain must dance on the house.
Tidying up, the old grandmother
hangs up the clever almanac

on its string. Birdlike, the almanac
hovers half open above the child,
hovers above the old grandmother
and her teacup full of dark brown tears.
She shivers and says she thinks the house
feels chilly, and puts more wood in the stove.

It was to be, says the Marvel Stove.
I know what I know, says the almanac.
With crayons the child draws a rigid house
and a winding pathway. Then the child
puts in a man with buttons like tears
and shows it proudly to the grandmother.

But secretly, while the grandmother
busies herself about the stove,
the little moons fall down like tears
from between the pages of the almanac
into the flower bed the child
has carefully placed in the front of the house.

Time to plant tears, says the almanac.
The grandmother sings to the marvellous stove
and the child draws another inscrutable house.

ELIZABETH BISHOP

121

OLD SALT KOSSABONE

Far back, related on my mother's side,
Old Salt Kossabone, I'll tell you how he died:
(Had been a sailor all his life—was nearly 90—lived with
    his married grandchild, Jenny;
House on a hill, with view of bay at hand, and distant
    cape, and stretch to open sea;)
The last of afternoon, the evening hours, for many a
    year his regular custom,
In his great arm chair by the window seated,
(Sometimes, indeed, through half the day,)
Watching the coming, going of the vessels, he mutters
    to himself
        —And now the close of all:
One struggling outbound brig, one day, baffled for
    long—cross-tides
        and much wrong going,
At last at nightfall strikes the breeze aright, her whole
    luck veering,
And swiftly bending round the cape, the darkness
    proudly entering,
        cleaving, as he watches,
"She's free—she's on her destination"—these the last
    words—
        when Jenny came, he sat there dead,
Dutch Kossabone, Old Salt, related on my mother's side,
    far back.

WALT WHITMAN

MY GRANDMOTHER

My grandmother moves to my mind in context of sorrow
And, as if apprehensive of near death, in black;
Whether erect in chair, her dry and corded throat
    harangued by grief,
Or at ragged book bent in Hebrew prayer,
Or gentle, submissive, and in tears to strangers;
Whether in sunny parlor or back of drawn blinds.

Though time and tongue made any love disparate,
On daguerreotype with classic perspective
Beauty I sigh and soften at is hers.
I pity her life of deaths, the agony of her own,
But most that history moved her through
Stranger lands and many houses,
Taking her exile for granted, confusing
The tongues and tasks of her children's children.

KARL SHAPIRO

A NEAR-PANTOUM FOR A BIRTHDAY

At my Grandmother's life I look,
In this my fiftieth year of age,
Not a recluse, like her, not dark,
Withdrawn; for love is my stage.

In this my fiftieth year of age,
I'll figure out my place, and not
Withdraw, for love is my stage;
Loving and loved in this green spot,

I'll single out my place, not
As she the suburb of despair
(Loving and loved in this green spot)
Who breathed the shadows of the air.

As she—the suburbs of despair,
The cold body, the cold heart,
Who breathed the shadows of the air,
Denying love, kept all apart.

The cold body, the cold heart!
May this next decade see my warmth
Preserving love in every part;
Let me be held in my love's arms!

May these next years contain my warmth—
At Grandmother's thin life I look—
Let me hold love, then, in my arms,
Not a recluse, all quick, not dark.

BARBARA HOWES

IN MEMORY OF MY DEAR GRANDCHILD ELIZABETH BRADSTREET WHO DECEASED AUGUST, 1665, BEING A YEAR AND HALF OLD

Farewell dear babe, my heart's too much content,
Farewell sweet babe, the pleasure of mine eye,
Fairwell fair flower that for a space was lent,
Then ta'en away unto eternity.
Blest babe, why should I once bewail thy fate,
Or sigh thy days so soon were terminate,
Sith thou art settled in an everlasting state.

2

By nature trees do rot when they are grown,
And plums and apples thoroughly ripe do fall,
And corn and grass are in their season mown,
And time brings down what is both strong and tall.
But plants new set to be eradicate,
And buds new blown to have so short a date,
Is by His hand alone that guides nature and fate.

ANNE BRADSTREET

125

TRUE KINDNESS IS A PURE DIVINE AFFINITY

True kindness is a pure divine affinity,
Not founded upon human consanguinity.
It is a spirit, not a blood relation,
Superior to family and station.

HENRY DAVID THOREAU

126

A father of the fatherless, and a judge of the widows,
  is God in his holy habitation.
God setteth the solitary in families.

PSALM 68:5, 6

OLD PEOPLE'S HOME

All are limitory, but each has her own
nuance of damage. The elite can dress and decent
themselves,
 are ambulant with a single stick, adroit
to read a book all through, or play the slow movements of
 easy sonatas. (Yet, perhaps their very
carnal freedom is their spirit's bane: intelligent
 of what has happened and why, they are obnoxious
to a glum beyond tears.) Then come those on wheels,
the average
 majority, who endure T.V. and, led by
lenient therapists, do community-singing, then
 the loners, muttering in Limbo, and last
the terminally incompetent, as improvident,
 unspeakable, impeccable as the plants
they parody. (Plants may sweat profusely but never
 sully themselves.) One tie, though, unites them: all
appeared when the world, though much was awry there,
was more
 spacious, more comely to look at, its Old Ones
with an audience and secular station. Then a child,
 in dismay with Mamma, could refuge with Gran
to be revalued and told a story. As of now,
 we all know what to expect, but their generation
is the first to fade like this, not at home but assigned
 to a numbered frequent ward, stowed out of
 conscience
as unpopular luggage.

As I ride the subway
to spend half-an-hour with one, I revisage
who she was in the pomp and sumpture of her hey-day,
when week-end visits were a presumptive joy,
not a good work. Am I cold to wish for a speedy
painless dormition, pray, as I know she prays,
that God or Nature will abrupt her earthly function?

W. H. AUDEN

CHILD TO PARENT

Honour thy father and thy mother,
as the Lord thy God hath
commanded thee; that thy days may
be prolonged, and that it may go
well with thee, in the land which the
Lord thy God giveth thee.

Deuteronomy 5:16

THE PRIMITIAE TO PARENTS

Our *Houshold-gods* our Parents be;
And manners good requires, that we
The first Fruits give to them, who gave
Us hands to get what here we have.

ROBERT HERRICK

Primitiæ: earliest products of the soil; first fruits; the first products of
a man's work

ABRAHAM'S KNIFE*

Where hills are hard and bare,
rocks like thrown dice, heat
and glare that's clean and pitiless,
a shadow dogs my heels, limp
as a drowned man washed ashore.
True sacrifice is secret, none
to applaud the ceremony, nor
witness to be moved to tears.
No one to see. God alone
knows, Whose great eye winks not,
from Whom no secrets are hid.

My father, I have loved you,
love you now, dead ten years.
Your ghost shadows me home.
Your laughter and your anger still
trouble my scarecrow head like wings.
My own children, my sons, study
my stranger's face. Their flesh,
bones frail as a small bird's,
is strange, too, in my hands.
What will become of us?
I read my murder in their eyes.

---

*Genesis 22:1-14

And you, old father, Abraham,
my judge and executioner, I pray
be witness to me now. I ask
some measure of your faith. Forgive
us, Jew and Gentile, all
your children, all your victims.
In naked country of no shadow
your hand is raised in shining arc.
And we are fountains of foolish tears
enough to flood and green a world again.
Strike for my heart. Your blade is light.

GEORGE GARRETT

THE CHANGELING

Toll no bell for me, dear Father, dear Mother,
      Waste no sighs;
There are my sisters, there is my little brother
   Who plays in the place called Paradise,
Your children all, your children for ever;
      But I, so wild,
Your disgrace, with the queer brown face, was never,
   Never, I know, but half your child!

In the garden at play, all day, last summer,
      Far and away I heard
The sweet "tweet-tweet" of a strange new-comer,
   The dearest, clearest call of a bird.
It lived down there in the deep green hollow,
   My own old home, and the fairies say
The word of a bird is a thing to follow,
   So I was away a night and a day.

One evening, too, by the nursery fire,
   We snuggled close and sat round so still,
When suddenly as the wind blew higher,
   Something scratched on the window-sill.
A pinched brown face peered in—I shivered;
   No one listened or seemed to see;
The arms of it waved and the wings of it quivered,
   Whoo—I knew it had come for me;
   Some are as bad as bad can be!
All night long they danced in the rain,
Round and round in a dripping chain,
Threw their caps at the window-pane,
   Tried to make me scream and shout
   And fling the bedclothes all about:

I meant to stay in bed that night,
And if only you had left a light
They would never have got me out.
   Sometimes I wouldn't speak, you see,
   Or answer when you spoke to me,
Because in the long, still dusks of Spring
You can hear the whole world whispering:
   The shy green grasses making love,
   The feathers grow on the dear, grey dove,
   The tiny heart of the redstart beat,
   The patter of the squirrel's feet,
The pebbles pushing in the silver streams,
The rushes talking in their dreams,
   The swish-swish of the bat's black wings,
   The wild-wood bluebell's sweet ting-tings,
   Humming and hammering at your ear,
      Everything there is to hear
In the heart of hidden things,
   But not in the midst of the nursery riot.
   That's why I wanted to be quiet,
      Couldn't do my sums, or sing,
      Or settle down to anything.
   And when, for that, I was sent upstairs
   I *did* kneel down to say my prayers;
But the King who sits on your high church steeple
Has nothing to do with us fairy people!

'Times I pleased you, dear Father, dear Mother,
   Learned all my lessons and liked to play,
And dearly I loved the little pale brother
   Whom some other bird must have called away.
Why did They bring me here to make me
   Not quite bad and not quite good,

Why, unless They're wicked, do They want, in spite,
        to take me
    Back to their wet, wild wood?
Now, every night I shall see the windows shining,
    The gold lamp's glow, and the fire's red gleam,
While the best of us are twining twigs and the rest of us
        are whining
        In the hollow by the stream.
Black and chill are Their nights on the wold;
    And They live so long and They feel no pain:
I shall grow up, but never grow old,
I shall always, always be very cold,
        I shall never come back again!

CHARLOTTE MEW

THE MOTHER

It was a noon of freedom,
an afternoon in chains,
and we have shared them, mother,
who fed me from your veins.

It was a long day's labor
that had no evening rest.
Sleep, can you sleep now, mother,
as once the babe at breast,

as once the babe within you,
sleep in the womb of earth?
Oh, take my blessing, mother,
for all I knew since birth:

sunlight and shadow, freedom
and prison, feast and dearth.
The cord was strong that bound us,
now binding me to earth.

MALCOLM COWLEY

THE WINTER OF THE SEPARATION

Where I grew up everything snowed:
from inches to feet of silence, falling
out of the ceiling, onto my bed.
When I came down with the chicken pox,
the field was mica under the phone wires
out the bathroom window. There was no shadow,
not any morning, save in the depth
of my bootprints. I was snowed in,
season on season, size six-and-a-half
in my ski boots, out under weighted pines
with my pheasant tracks and the rabbit stains.
Mothers didn't have skis in that ice age,
my father was always away, and there
never was wind where I drifted, up
to my waist in igloos. Once, through small snow,
my mother came out in her own new flurry
to call me home: she held out the back
of a black kid glove to let one crystal settle.
She explained, she tried to explain, all sides.
When her hand barely touched me, I melted.

PHILIP BOOTH

THE DIVORCE

Mother, dear, was it just a year
That I saw him every day?
He got me up each morning;
I knew no other way.

I never quite remember
His face now he is gone—
His touch of hand upon me,
His laughter and his song.

Once time meant nothing to me,
But I have learned to tell—
By months, by weeks, by hours—
The moment of arrival—the moment
    of farewell.

PAMELA CRAWFORD HOLAHAN

from KADDISH

Another year, I left NY—on West Coast in
Berkeley cottage dreamed of her soul—that, thru life, in
what form it stood in that body, ashen or manic, gone
beyond joy—

near its death—with eyes—was my own love in its
form, the Naomi, my mother on earth still—sent her long
letter—& wrote hymns to the mad—Work of the
merciful Lord of Poetry.

that causes the broken grass to be green, or the
rock to break in grass—or the Sun to be constant to earth
—Sun of all sunflowers and days on bright iron bridges—
what shines on old hospitals—as on my yard—

Returning from San Francisco one night,
Orlovsky in my room—Whalen in his peaceful chair—a
telegram from Gene, Naomi dead—

Outside I bent my head to the ground under the
bushes near the garage—knew she was better—

at last—not left to look on Earth alone—2 years of
solitude—no one, at age nearing 60—old woman of skulls

Kaddish: the Hebrew prayer for the dead

—once long-tressed Naomi of Bible—

or Ruth who wept in America—Rebecca aged in Newark—David remembering his Harp, now lawyer at Yale

or Svul Avrum—Israel Abraham—myself—to sing in the wilderness toward God—O Elohim!—so to the end —2 days after her death I got her letter—

Strange Prophecies anew! She wrote—'The key is in the window, the key is in the sunlight at the window —I have the key—Get married Allen don't take drugs— the key is in the bars, in the sunlight in the window.

Love,
your mother'

which is Naomi—

ALLEN GINSBERG

THE BURIAL

for Martha Hillard MacLeish

Life relinquishing, by life relinquished—
Oh but the young tart quick beating
Life in your heart, my mother—Oh and sweet—
Where will they put that down among these mingled
Soot-stained grave-stones here? Or do they think
The thirst is gone now and the apple eaten?
Do they think the journeys, like your feet,
Are still? And is it so? The one, the single
Answer that the bird makes to the hill—
Had your heart, asking, heard it? Was it done?
Life you never finished, did your life
Finish, my mother? Was all suddenly still,
All understood, all answered and all one:
Young girl, old woman, widow, mother, wife?

ARCHIBALD MAC LEISH

from THE AURORAS OF AUTUMN

Farewell to an idea . . . The mother's face,
The purpose of the poem, fills the room.
They are together, here, and it is warm,

With none of the prescience of oncoming dreams,
It is evening. The house is evening, half dissolved.
Only the half they can never possess remains,

Still-starred. It is the mother they possess,
Who gives transparence to their present peace.
She makes that gentler that can gentle be.

And yet she too is dissolved, she is destroyed.
She gives transparence. But she has grown old.
The necklace is a carving not a kiss.

The soft hands are a motion not a touch.
The house will crumble and the books will burn.
They are at ease in a shelter of the mind

And the house is of the mind and they and time,
Together, all together. Boreal night
Will look like frost as it approaches them

And to the mother as she falls asleep
And as they say good-night, good-night. Upstairs
The windows will be lighted, not the rooms.

A wind will spread its windy grandeurs round
And knock like a rifle-butt against the door.
The wind will command them with invincible sound.

WALLACE STEVENS

145

from BETWEEN THE PORCH AND THE ALTAR

Mother and Son

Meeting his mother makes him lose ten years,
Or is it twenty? Time, no doubt, has ears
That listen to the swallowed serpent, wound
Into its bowels, but he thinks no sound
Is possible before her, he thinks the past
Is settled. It is honest to hold fast
Merely to what one sees with one's own eyes
When the red velvet curves and haunches rise
To blot him from the pretty driftwood fire's
Façade of welcome. Then the son retires
Into the sack and selfhood of the boy
Who clawed through fallen houses of his Troy,
Homely and human only when the flames
Crackle in recollection. Nothing shames
Him more than this uncoiling, counterfeit
Body presented as an idol. It
Is something in a circus, big as life,
The painted dragon, a mother and a wife
With flat glass eyes pushed at him on a stick;
The human mover crawls to make them click.
The forehead of her father's portrait peels
With rosy dryness, and the schoolboy kneels
To ask the benediction of the hand,
Lifted as though to motion him to stand,
Dangling its watch-chain on the Holy Book—
A little golden snake that mouths a hook.

ROBERT LOWELL

146

UNREALIZED

Down comes the winter rain—
      Spoils my hat and bow—
Runs into the poll of me;
      But mother won't know.

We've been out and caught a cold,
      Knee-deep in snow;
Such a lucky thing it is
      That mother won't know!

Rosy lost herself last night—
      Couldn't tell where to go.
Yes—it rather frightened her,
      But mother didn't know.

Somebody made Willy drunk
      At the Christmas show:
O 'twas fun! It's well for him
      That mother won't know!

Howsoever wild we are,
      Late at school or slow,
Mother won't be cross with us,
      Mother won't know.

How we cried the day she died!
      Neighbours whispering low.
But we now do what we will—
      Mother won't know.

THOMAS HARDY

THE HORSE SHOW

Constantly near you, I never in my entire
sixty-four years knew you so well as yesterday
or half so well. We talked. You were never
so lucid, so disengaged from all exigencies
of place and time. We talked of ourselves,
intimately, a thing never heard of between us.
How long have we waited? almost a hundred years.

You said, Unless there is some spark, some
spirit we keep within ourselves, life, a
continuing life's impossible—and it is all
we have. There is no other life, only the one.
The world of the spirits that comes afterward
is the same as our own, just like you sitting
there they come and talk to me, just the same.

They come to bother us. Why? I said. I don't
know. Perhaps to find out what we are doing.
Jealous, do you think? I don't know. I
don't know why they should want to come back.
I was reading about some men who had been
buried under a mountain, I said to her, and
one of them came back after two months,

digging himself out. It was in Switzerland,
you remember? Of course I remember. The
villagers tho't it was a ghost coming down
to complain. They were frightened. They
do come, she said, what you call
my "visions." I talk to them just as I
am talking to you. I see them plainly.

Oh if I could only read! You don't know
what adjustments I have made. All
I can do is to try to live over again
what I knew when your brother and you
were children—but I can't always succeed.
Tell me about the horse show. I have
been waiting all week to hear about it.

Mother darling, I wasn't able to get away.
Oh that's too bad. It was just a show;
they make the horses walk up and down
to judge them by their form. Oh is that
all? I tho't it was something else. Oh
they jump and run too. I wish you had been
there, I was so interested to hear about it.

WILLIAM CARLOS WILLIAMS

A WOMAN MOURNED
BY DAUGHTERS

Now, not a tear begun,
we sit here in your kitchen,
spent, you see, already.
You are swollen till you strain
this house and the whole sky.
You, whom we so often
succeeded in ignoring!
You are puffed up in death
like a corpse pulled from the sea;
we groan beneath your weight.
And yet you were a leaf,
a straw blown on the bed,
you had long since become
crisp as a dead insect.
What is it, if not you,
that settles on us now
like satin you pulled down
over our bridal heads?
What rises in our throats
like food you prodded in?
Nothing could be enough.
You breathe upon us now
through solid assertions
of yourself: teaspoons, goblets,
seas of carpet, a forest
of old plants to be watered,
an old man in an adjoining
room to be touched and fed.
And all this universe
dares us to lay a finger
anywhere, save exactly
as you would wish it done.

ADRIENNE RICH

MOTHERS

for J.B.

Oh mother,
here in your lap,
as good as a bowlful of clouds,
I your greedy child
am given your breast,
the sea wrapped in skin,
and your arms,
roots covered with moss
and with new shoots sticking out
to tickle the laugh out of me.
Yes, I am wedded to my teddy
but he has the smell of you
as well as the smell of me.
Your necklace that I finger
is all angel eyes.
Your rings that sparkle
are like the moon on the pond.
Your legs that bounce me up and down,
your dear nylon-covered legs,
are the horses I will ride
into eternity.

Oh mother,
after this lap of childhood
I will never go forth
into the big people's world
as an alien,
a fabrication,
or falter
when someone else
is as empty as a shoe.

ANNE SEXTON

151

FATHER'S VOICE

"No need to get home early;
the car can see in the dark."
　　He wanted me to be rich
　　the only way we could,
　　easy with what we had.

And always that was his gift,
given for me ever since,
　　easy gift, a wind
　　that keeps on blowing for flowers
　　or birds wherever I look.

World, I am your slow guest,
one of the common things
　　that move in the sun and have
　　close, reliable friends
　　in the earth, in the air, in the rock.

WILLIAM STAFFORD

YOUTH

Strange bird,
His song remains secret.
He worked too hard to read books.
He never heard how Sherwood Anderson
Got out of it, and fled to Chicago, furious to free himself
From his hatred of factories.
My father toiled fifty years
At Hazel-Atlas Glass,
Caught among girders that smash the kneecaps
Of dumb honyaks.
Did he shudder with hatred in the cold shadow of grease?
Maybe. But my brother and I do know
He came home as quiet as the evening.

He will be getting dark, soon,
And loom through new snow.
I know his ghost will drift home
To the Ohio River, and sit down, alone,
Whittling a root.
He will say nothing.
The waters flow past, older, younger
Than he is, or I am.

JAMES WRIGHT

TO MY FATHER

Peace and her huge invasion to these shores
Puts daily home; innumerable sails
Dawn on the far horizon and draw near;
Innumerable loves, uncounted hopes
To our wild coasts, not darkling now, approach:
Not now obscure, since thou and thine are there,
And bright on the lone isle, the foundered reef,
The long, resounding foreland, Pharos stands.

These are thy works, O father, these thy crown;
Whether on high the air be pure, they shine
Along the yellowing sunset, and all night
Among the unnumbered stars of God they shine;
Or whether fogs arise and far and wide
The low sea-level drown—each finds a tongue
And all night long the tolling bell resounds:
So shine, so toll, till night be overpast,
Till the stars vanish, till the sun return,
And in the haven rides the fleet secure.

In the first hour, the seaman in his skiff
Moves through the unmoving bay, to where the town
Its earliest smoke into the air upbreathes,
And the rough hazels climb along the beach.
To the tugg'd oar the distant echo speaks.
The ship lies resting, where by reef and roost
Thou and thy lights have led her like a child.

This hast thou done, and I—can I be base?
I must arise, O father, and to port
Some lost, complaining seaman pilot home.

ROBERT LOUIS STEVENSON

R.L.S.'s father was an architect of lighthouses.

THOSE WINTER SUNDAYS

Sundays too my father got up early
and put his clothes on in the blueblack cold,
then with cracked hands that ached
from labor in the weekday weather made
banked fires blaze. No one ever thanked him.

I'd wake and hear the cold splintering, breaking.
When the rooms were warm, he'd call,
and slowly I would rise and dress,
fearing the chronic angers of that house,

Speaking indifferently to him,
who had driven out the cold
and polished my good shoes as well.
What did I know, what did I know
of love's austere and lonely offices?

ROBERT HAYDEN

OTTO

1

He was the youngest son of a strange brood,
A Prussian who learned early to be rude
To fools and frauds: He does not put on airs
Who lived above a potting shed for years.
I think of him, and I think of his men,
As close to him as any kith or kin.
Max Laurisch had the greenest thumb of all.
A florist does not woo the beautiful:
He potted plants as if he hated them.
What root of his ever denied its stem?
When flowers grew, their bloom extended him.

2

His hand could fit into a woman's glove,
And in a wood he knew whatever moved;
Once when he saw two poachers on his land,
He threw his rifle over with one hand;
Dry bark flew in their faces from his shot,—
He always knew what he was aiming at.
They stood there with their guns; he walked toward,
Without his rifle, and slapped each one hard;
It was no random act, for those two men
Had slaughtered game, and cut young fir trees down.
I was no more than seven at the time.

3

A house for flowers! House upon house they built,
Whether for love or out of obscure guilt
For ancestors who loved a warlike show,
Or Frenchmen killed a hundred years ago,
And yet still violent men, whose stacked-up guns
Killed every cat that neared their pheasant runs;
When Hattie Wright's angora died as well,
My father took it to her, by the tail.
Who loves the small can be both saint and boor,
(And some grow out of shape, their seed impure;)
The Indians loved him, and the Polish poor.

4

In my mind's eye I see those fields of glass,
As I looked out at them from the high house,
Riding beneath the moon, hid from the moon,
Then slowly breaking whiter in the dawn;
When George the watchman's lantern dropped from
    sight
The long pipes knocked: it was the end of night.
I'd stand upon my bed, a sleepless child
Watching the waking of my father's world.—
O world so far away! O my lost world!

THEODORE ROETHKE

THE HOSPITAL WINDOW

I have just come down from my father.
Higher and higher he lies
Above me in a blue light
Shed by a tinted window.
I drop through six white floors
And then step out onto pavement.

Still feeling my father ascend,
I start to cross the firm street,
My shoulder blades shining with all
The glass the huge building can raise.
Now I must turn round and face it,
And know his one pane from the others.

Each window possesses the sun
As though it burned there on a wick.
I wave, like a man catching fire.
All the deep-dyed windowpanes flash,
And, behind them, all the white rooms
They turn to the color of Heaven.

Ceremoniously, gravely, and weakly,
Dozens of pale hands are waving
Back, from inside their flames.
Yet one pure pane among these
Is the bright, erased blankness of nothing.
I know that my father is there,

In the shape of his death still living.
The traffic increases around me
Like a madness called down on my head.
The horns blast at me like shotguns,
And drivers lean out, driven crazy—
But now my propped-up father

Lifts his arm out of stillness at last.
The light from the window strikes me
And I turn as blue as a soul,
As the moment when I was born.
I am not afraid for my father—
Look! He is grinning; he is not

Afraid for my life, either,
As the wild engines stand at my knees
Shredding their gears and roaring,
And I hold each car in its place
For miles, inciting its horn
To blow down the walls of the world

That the dying may float without fear
In the bold blue gaze of my father.
Slowly I move to the sidewalk
With my pin-tingling hand half dead
At the end of my bloodless arm.
I carry it off in amazement,

High, still higher, still waving,
My recognized face fully mortal,
Yet not; not at all, in the pale,
Drained, otherworldly, stricken,
Created hue of stained glass.
I have just come down from my father.

JAMES DICKEY

≥ *159*

TWO POSTURES BESIDE A FIRE

1

Tonight I watch my father's hair,
As he sits dreaming near his stove.
Knowing my feather of despair,
He sent me an owl's plume for love,
Lest I not know, so I've come home.
Tonight Ohio, where I once
Hounded and cursed my loneliness,
Shows me my father, who broke stones,
Wrestled and mastered great machines,
And rests, shadowing his lovely face.

2

Nobly his hands fold together in his repose.
He is proud of me, believing
I have done strong things among men and become a man
Of place among men of place in the large cities.
I will not waken him.
I have come home alone, without wife or child
To delight him. Awake, solitary and welcome,
I too sit near his stove, the lines
Of an ugly age scarring my face, and my hands
Twitch nervously about.

JAMES WRIGHT

FATHER

I dreamed my father flicked
in his grave
then like a fish in water
wrestled with the ground
surfaced and wandered:
I could not find him
through woods, roots, mires
in his bad shape: and
when I found him he was
dead again and had to be
re-entered in the ground:
I said to my mother I still
have you: but out of the
dream I know she died
sixteen years before his
first death:
as I become a child again
a longing that will go away
only with my going grows.

A. R. AMMONS

ELEGY FOR MY FATHER

Father, whom I murdered every night but one,
That one, when your death murdered me,
Your body waits within the wasting sod.
Clutching at the straw-face of your God,
Do you remember me, your morbid son,
Curled in a death, all motive unbegun,
Continuum of flesh, who never thought to be
The mourning mirror of your potency?

All you had battled for the nightmare took
Away, as dropping from your eyes, the sea-
Salt tears, with messages that none could read,
Impotent, pellucid, were the final seeds
You sowed. Above you, the white night nurse shook
His head, and moaning on the moods of luck,
We knew the double-dealing enemy:
From pain you suffered, pain had set you free.

Down from the ceiling, father, circles came:
Angels, perhaps, to bear your soul away.
But tasting the persisting salt of pain,
I think my tears created them, though in vain,
Like yours, they fell. All losses link: the same
Creature marred us both to stake his claim.
Shutting my eyelids, barring night and day,
I saw, and see, your body borne away.

Two months dead, I wrestle with your name
Whose separate letters make a paltry sum
That is not you. If still you harbor mine,
Think of the house we had in summertime,
When in the sea-light every early game
Was played with love, and if death's waters came,
You'd rescue me. How I would take you from,
Now, if I could, its whirling vacuum.

HOWARD MOSS

MY FATHER'S FACE

Old he was but not yet wax,
old and old but not yet gray.
What an awkwardness of facts
gray and waxen when he lay.

Rage had held me forty years,
only five have sought his grace.
Will my disproportionate tears
quell at last his smiling face?

Awkwardly at his behest
I this queer rhyme try to make
after one that he loved best,
made long since by Willy Blake.

HAYDEN CARRUTH

MY FATHER'S DEATH

After the laboring birth, the clean stripped hull
Glides down the ways and is gently set free,
The landlocked, launched; the cramped made bountiful—
Oh, grave great moment when ships take the sea!
Alone now in my life, no longer child,
This hour and its flood of mystery,
Where death and love are wholly reconciled,
Launches the ship of all my history.
Accomplished now is the last struggling birth,
I have slipped out from the embracing shore
Nor look for comfort to maternal earth.
I shall not be a daughter any more,
But through this final parting, all stripped down,
Launched on the tide of love, go out full grown.

MAY SARTON

ROWING IN LINCOLN PARK

You are, in 1925, my father;
Straw-hatted, prim, I am your only son;
Through zebra-light fanwise on the lagoon
Our rented boat slides on the lucent calm.

And we are wistful, having come to this
First tableau of ourselves: your eyes that look
Astonished on my nine bravado years,
My conscious heart that hears the oar-locks click

And swells with facts particular to you—
How France is pink, how noon is shadowless,
How bad unruly angels tumbled from
That ivory eminence, and how they burned.

And you are vaguely undermined and plan
Surprise of pennies, some directed gesture,
Being proud and inarticulate, your mind
Dramatic and unpoised, surprised with love.

In silences hermetical as this
The lean ancestral hand returns, the voice
Of unfulfillment with its blade-like touch
Warning our scattered breath to be resolved.

And sons and fathers in their mutual eyes,
Exchange (a moment huge and volatile)
The glance of paralytics, or the news
Of master-builders on the trespassed earth.

Now I am twenty-two and you are dead,
And late in Lincoln Park the rowers cross
Unfavored in their odysseys, the lake
Not dazzling nor wide, but dark and commonplace.

JOHN MALCOLM BRINNIN

if there are any heavens my mother will(all by herself)have
one. It will not be a pansy heaven nor
a fragile heaven of lilies-of-the-valley but
it will be a heaven of blackred roses

my father will be(deep like a rose
tall like a rose)

standing near my

(swaying over her
silent)
with eyes which are really petals and see

nothing with the face of a poet really which
is a flower and not a face with
hands
which whisper
This is my beloved my

                  (suddenly in sunlight

he will bow,

& the whole garden will bow)

                       E. E. CUMMINGS

from *CHANGING MIND*

My father which art in earth
From whom I got my birth,
What is it that I inherit?
From the bones fallen apart
And the deciphered heart,
Body and spirit.

My mother which art in tomb
Who carriedst me in thy womb,
What is it that I inherit?
From the thought come to dust
And the remembered lust,
Body and spirit.

Father and mother, who gave
Life, love, and now the grave,
What is it that I can be?
Nothing but what lies here,
The hand still, the brain sere,
Naught lives in thee

Nor ever will live, save
It have within this grave
Roots in the mingled heart,
In the damp ashes wound
Where the past, underground,
Falls, falls apart.

CONRAD AIKEN

169

AT NIGHT

In the dust are my father's beautiful hands,
In the dust are my mother's eyes.
Here by the shore of the ocean standing,
Watching: still I do not understand.

Love flows over me, around me,
Here at night by the sea, by the sovereign sea.

Gone is that bone-hoard of strength;
Gone her gentle motion laughing, walking.

Is it not strange that disease and death
Should rest, by the undulant sea?

And I stare, rich with gifts, alone,

Feeling from the sea those terrene presences,
My father's hands, my mother's eyes.

RICHARD EBERHART

INDEX TO AUTHORS

INDEX TO TITLES

INDEX TO FIRST LINES

ACKNOWLEDGMENTS

Thanks are due to the following for permission to include copyrighted poems:

Atheneum Publishers, Inc., for "Sire from *The Moving Target* by W. S. Merwin, Copyright © 1962, 1963 by W. S. Merwin; and "Elegy for My Father" from *Selected Poems* by Howard Moss, Copyright © 1954, 1971 by Howard Moss ("Elegy for My Father" was first published in *The New Yorker*).

John Malcolm Brinnin for "Rowing in Lincoln Park."

Jonathan Cape Ltd. and the Executors of the Estate of C. Day Lewis, for "My Mother's Sister" from *The Room* by C. Day Lewis.

City Lights for the selection from "Kaddish" from *Kaddish and Other Poems* by Allen Ginsberg, Copyright © 1961 by Allen Ginsberg.

Curtis Brown, Ltd., for "The Mother" from *The Collected Poems of Babette Deutsch*, Copyright © 1969 by Babette Deutsch.

Andre Deutsch Limited for "Ancestors" from *Collected Poems* by Roy Fuller.

Doubleday & Company, Inc., for "Elegy," Copyright © 1955 by New Republic, Inc., "Wish for a Young Wife" and "Otto," both Copyright © 1963 by Beatrice Roethke as Administratrix of the Estate of Theodore Roethke, all from the book *The Collected Poems of Theodore Roethke*.

Gerald Duckworth & Co., Ltd., for "The Changeling" from *Collected Poems* of Charlotte Mew, Copyright © 1953 by Estate of C. Mew.

Farrar, Straus & Giroux, Inc., for "Loss" from *Henry's Fate and Other Poems* by John Berryman, Copyright © 1969 by John Berryman, Copyright © 1975, 1976, 1977 by Kate Berryman; "Manners" and "Sestina" from *The Complete Poems* by Elizabeth Bishop, Copyright © 1955, 1956 by Elizabeth Bishop; "To My Brother" from *The Blue Estuaries* by Louise Bogan, Copyright © 1935, 1963, 1968 by Louise Bogan; "The Old Flame" from *For the Union Dead* by Robert Lowell, Copyright © 1962, 1964 by Robert Lowell; and "Adaptation of a Theme by Catullus" from *Allen Tate Collected Poems*

Edited by Helen Plotz

THOMAS Y. CROWELL CO.

The Earth Is the Lord's:
Poems of the Spirit

Imagination's Other Place:
Poems of Science and Mathematics

Poems from the German

Poems of Emily Dickinson

Poems of Robert Louis Stevenson

Untune the Sky:
Poems of Music and the Dance

The Marvelous Light:
Poets and Poetry

MACMILLAN PUBLISHING CO., INC.

The Pinnacled Tower
Selected Poems of Thomas Hardy

GREENWILLOW BOOKS

As I Walked Out One Evening:
A Book of Ballads

The Gift Outright:
America to Her Poets

Life Hungers to Abound
Poems of the Family